WHEN GOD ANSWERS PRAYER

WHEN GOD ANSWERS PRAYER

BOB RUSSELL

WITH RUSTY RUSSELL

HOWARD PUBLISHING CO.

Our purpose at Howard Publishing is to:
- *Increase faith* in the hearts of growing Christians
- *Inspire holiness* in the lives of believers
- *Instill hope* in the hearts of struggling people everywhere
Because He's coming again!

Published by Howard Publishing Co., Inc.,
3117 North 7th Street, West Monroe, Louisiana 71291-2227

03 04 05 06 07 08 09 10 11 12   10 9 8 7 6 5 4 3 2 1

Library of Congress Cataloging-in-Publication Data
    Russell, Bob, 1943-
        [text forthcoming]
        ISBN: 978-1-4516-7623-5
        [text forthcoming]

Edited by Dawn M. Brandon and Tammy L. Bicket
Interior design by John Luke

To my mom, Catherine Russell

I'm so glad God answered your prayers!

CONTENTS

CONTENTS

ACKNOWLEDGMENTS

If this book touches anyone's life in a positive way, the people who deserve the greatest credit are the dozens of Southeast Christian Church members and friends who shared with us their stories of answered prayer or told us of their continued faith in a good God when God didn't answer. I wish we could have shared every letter.

Once again we owe a debt of gratitude to our fellow staff members: Dave Stone, Dave Kennedy, and Kyle Idleman contributed illustrations for this book, along with our friend and fellow preacher Mark Jones from Columbus, Indiana. Debbie Carper and Dana Pinkston are the pillars of the office and are so patient when sermon or book deadlines are approaching! And Cameron McDonald worked hard to see that the footnotes and finest details were done with excellence.

It's an honor to publish another book with our friends Denny and Philis Boultinghouse at Howard Publishing.

ACKNOWLEDGMENTS

Thanks for assigning Dawn Brandon and Tammy Bicket again to be our editors! She's a joy to work with.

Though a majority of what you read in this book has been said by me in a sermon at one point or another, my son Rusty is the one who suffers to put it down on paper, fill in the gaps, and make it flow together in a literary style. And Rusty is the one who feels the pressure to get it done by deadline day. So Rusty says,

> I want to thank Kellie, Charlie, Tommy, and Kimberly, who gave up several months' worth of "Daddy time" while the book was being put together and ministry and school weren't able to be put on hold. And I need to thank Charlie Booth, Chris Hadley, Rich Young, and all my other friends who prayed for us; and Dan and Stacy Small—without your help in a bind, I would never have met the deadline!

My wife, Judy, has sacrificed every week for thirty-eight years of ministry. Thanks, Judy! And Phil and Lisa and Corrie, we're so proud of you for keeping the faith even when God hasn't answered all our prayers.

Thank you, God, for answering most of them. To God be the glory.

INTRODUCTION

I'm honored that Howard Publishing asked me to write this book about answered prayer. On one hand, I can understand why they would ask me, because few pastors have witnessed more consistent, dramatic answers to prayer than I have. In four decades of ministry I've seen more lost people saved, sick people restored, threatened homes unified, worship services anointed, barren wombs opened, money raised, and buildings built than almost any other preacher I know.

But on the other hand, I feel like I'm the least likely person to talk about prayer, because I'm not very good at it. I believe in prayer, and I think my life reflects that. Every morning I have a devotional time when I kneel and pray, and I think I can even understand what Paul meant when he said we should pray without ceasing. I pray regularly, and I've witnessed many answers. But I still don't consider myself an expert at prayer. I'm not gifted at prayer like some people are. The Bible commands everyone to sing, but some are more gifted singers than others. We are all commanded to evangelize, but some find it easy while others struggle. We're all commanded to pray, but there are some people for whom prayer is as natural as breathing. It just flows out of them as a part of their Christian life.

My friend Russ Blowers is gifted to pray. I recently phoned Russ, a retired preacher who lives in Indianapolis. He wasn't in, so I got his voice mail. The message wasn't a greeting—it was a prayer! When you call Russ and get his voice mail, his recorded voice answers in an upbeat tone:

> Heavenly Father, I thank you that when we call upon you, we never get an answering machine! But I pray for this person who is calling me. May this be one of the best days of his or her life! Help them to be patient with me, because I can hardly wait to call them back. In Jesus' name, amen.

If I did something like that, it would sound corny. But coming from Russ, it's natural and genuine. His upbeat tone is even more impressive when you know the difficult circumstances he is experiencing now. Russ's wife is in the final stages of Alzheimer's disease. Yet despite these circumstances, he is praying for other people—even on his voice mail! I hear his message and feel convicted. If you call my answering machine, you'll get something like, "This is Bob. Leave a message, and keep it brief!"

Maybe you're a prayer plodder like me. You do it because you believe in it, but it doesn't come easily. You find yourself trying to remain vigilant, but you usually feel your prayer life is lacking. If so, I hope we can learn something together about prayer as we study God's Word and listen to the testimonies of others.

If you are gifted at prayer, praise God! I hope this book will reinforce what you know to be true. I'm confident you will be inspired by the true stories of answered prayer. And I'm sure your faith will be strengthened by the authentic testimonies of those who have remained faithful to God despite unanswered prayers.

There are dozens of excellent books on how to pray. This is not another how-to-pray book. I believe that if I can convince you of prayer's effectiveness, you will find a way to pray more efficiently. If I said to you, "I started going to a chiropractor, and it really helped my back pain," I wouldn't have to teach you how to find a chiropractor. All I have to do is convince you of the practitioner's effectiveness, and you'll find a way to talk to him or her. I hope this book convinces you that prayer works and motivates you to find a way to talk to the Great Physician yourself.

Maybe you read about a committed Christian named George Mueller who kept a journal of his prayers for more than fifty years. After he died, his children found boxes and boxes full of his journals. As they began to leaf through the journals, they saw that many of the sections had been underlined. They realized that the underscoring represented the many answered prayers he had witnessed. Mueller's children were determined to count how many answered prayers their father had underlined, so each sibling took a number of the journals and agreed to return on a certain date to discuss what they had found.

When the family got back together, they discovered that George Mueller had underlined fifty thousand answers to prayer—that's a thousand answers a year, almost three answers a day, for fifty years! What an incredible amount of faith he had! Most of us don't even ask three different things of God each day, let alone record all his answers.

Jesus said, "When you pray, go into your room, close the door and pray to your Father, who is unseen. Then your Father, who sees what is done in secret, will reward you" (Matthew 6:6). That's the simple message of this book. Prayer works. When you talk to the Father, he rewards you. Even if it doesn't come easily—even if some of your prayers are not answered the way you hoped they would be—God rewards sincere prayer. Prayer is the channel through which God pours out his blessings on us. You may never be as great a prayer warrior as George Mueller was. But I hope reading this book will inspire you to start believing in the power of prayer and begin to make your own prayer list with underlines.

May God answer your prayers!

Part One

GOD ANSWERS PRAYER

Chapter One

PRAYER CHANGES GOD'S MIND

*God will do nothing on earth except
in answer to believing prayer.*
—John Wesley

God was angry. So angry that he was ready to destroy his chosen ones. "They are a stiff-necked people," the Lord said to Moses. "Now leave me alone so that my anger may burn against them and that I may destroy them. Then I will make you into a great nation" (Exodus 32:9–10).

Who could blame him? The people deserved it. Justice demanded it. How could they mock God after all he had done for them?

The Lord had etched the Ten Commandments on stone tablets, but before Moses could even deliver them, the first two had already been broken—big time—by every one of the Israelites as they rebelled against God. At the people's request, Aaron had taken their gold and fashioned an idol—a calf, like one of the statues they'd seen the Egyptians worship. Then they mocked the holy name of God by daring to worship the golden calf. They even had the gall to say that

3

this statue was responsible for their newfound freedom! How ungrateful they were! God's anger boiled.

Moses was taken aback. He didn't want to see his brother and all the people of Israel destroyed. But what could he do? The God of the universe had spoken.

Still, Moses couldn't help himself. He prayed a desperate prayer of intercession on behalf of the Israelite people, hoping against hope that he could change God's mind.

> "O LORD," he said, "why should your anger burn against your people, whom you brought out of Egypt with great power and a mighty hand? Why should the Egyptians say, 'It was with evil intent that he brought them out, to kill them in the mountains and to wipe them off the face of the earth'? Turn from your fierce anger; relent and do not bring disaster on your people. Remember your servants Abraham, Isaac and Israel, to whom you swore by your own self: 'I will make your descendants as numerous as the stars in the sky and I will give your descendants all this land I promised them, and it will be their inheritance forever.'" (Exodus 32:11–13)

It was gutsy. Who was Moses to think he could alter the mind of God? But the Bible reports an amazing thing: *Because of the prayer of Moses, God changed his mind.* The next verse says it simply: "The LORD relented and did not bring on his people the disaster he had threatened" (Exodus 32:14).

The children of Israel still suffered severe consequences for their actions. Three thousand people died for their crimes against God. But tens of thousands escaped certain annihilation, and the children of Israel continued as a

4

nation because Moses prayed that God would change his mind—and God answered.

CAN GOD'S MIND REALLY BE CHANGED?

This amazing story presents a challenge to those who believe that God predestines everything that happens. I don't know exactly how to reconcile God's foreknowledge with the free will of man, but the Bible says clearly that God changed his mind as a result of Moses' prayer.

Some people would contend that God's mind can't really be changed if he knows and controls the future. They say this story about Moses may be real, but God only symbolically changed his mind in order to test Moses' resolve to lead the people, or to test his faith in God's goodness.

God is sovereign and certainly doesn't *have* to change his mind, but the Bible says he did, and the Scripture is full of other examples of God's changing his mind—with Abraham, Elijah, and Hezekiah, just to name a few. James tells us that the prayer of a righteous person is "powerful and effective" (James 5:16). It's not just a mirage—prayer has real power.[1]

Theologians tend to go to one of two extremes to explain this. Some hyper-Calvinists want to explain away all the Scripture passages indicating that God allows the actions of man to change the future. But that would make us mere puppets in a robotic world created by a dictator, and that's not at all what Scripture teaches.

Today, a new teaching at the opposite extreme is gaining popularity. These so-called open theists say that God possesses a progressive will—that he knows the present and can predict the future, but he doesn't know the future *for sure*. This teaching allows for God's mind to be changed by prayer, but it isn't biblical. It's a dangerous heresy.[2] The Bible says that God knows and controls the future, but he allows the prayers of men to play a role in determining exactly what that future will be.

God doesn't always change his mind just because we pray. God is sovereign: He knows and controls the future. But the Bible says that somehow—we don't know how—God sometimes allows our prayers to affect future events.

GOD HAS MIDDLE KNOWLEDGE

In trying to understand these things, it's helpful to consider that God has what some theologians have called "middle knowledge." God not only knows the future, but he knows *all possible futures*. If God is all-powerful and all-knowing, then God can know both possible futures in Moses' case. God knows what will happen if Moses appeals for leniency and what will happen if he doesn't pray at all. And although God also knows which "possible future" is going to be the real one, this helps us understand how prayer can truly make a difference. God is so powerful that he can allow us to affect the future with our prayers, yet still work out his ultimate plan for this world because he not only knows the future, he knows all possible futures. It's kind of dizzying, but the bottom line is, prayer works!

Let me see if I can illustrate this with a scene from the old movie *Back to the Future, Part 2*. In the film Doc Brown and Marty travel from their present (1985) to the future—the year 2015—to correct some problems with Marty's kids. Unbeknownst to them, the antagonist, Biff (an old man in 2015), steals the time machine and returns to the 1950s to deliver a sports almanac to his younger self. Then he returns to the future without anyone knowing what transpired.

When Doc and Marty return to 1985, the world is in chaos. Riots and shootings are everywhere. Biff, who in 1956 had become "the luckiest man ever" (because he possessed a sports almanac from the future, telling him the results of every major sporting event), has taken over the town, legalized gambling, and erected monuments to himself. Marty asks Doc what happened.

"Obviously, the time continuum has been disrupted, creating this now temporal events sequence, resulting in this alternate reality," Doc says.

"English, Doc!" Marty demands.

"Here, let me illustrate," Doc says as he reaches for a blackboard. "Imagine that this line represents time." He draws a line across the board. "Here's the present—1985—Future—Past." He draws 1985 in the middle and the word "Future" at the right end, "Past" at the left end. "Prior to this point in time [Doc points to the present], somewhere in the past, the time line skewed into this tangent, creating an alternate 1985." Doc then draws another time line, jutting out from the past.

He explains that the alternate time line is "alternate to you, me, and Einstein [his dog], but reality to everyone else."

After a little research, they discover that Biff had stolen the sports almanac and the time machine while they were in the future and had given the almanac to the young Biff somewhere in the past. "OK, Doc," Marty says. "We go back to the future, and we stop Biff from stealing the time machine."

An animated Doc Brown responds:

> We can't! Because if we travel into the future from this point in time [he points to the "1985" on the alternate time line], it will be the future of this reality [underlines the alternate time line]—in which Biff is corrupt and powerful and married to your mother!...No, our only chance to repair the present is in the past, at the point where the time line skewed into this tangent. In order to put the universe back as we remember it and get back to our reality, we have to find out the exact date and the specific circumstances of how, where, and when young Biff got his hands on that sports almanac.[3]

One of the lessons in the *Back to the Future* series is that every little change in the past affects the future. Each decision, each action, creates an "alternate time line" in addition to the one that would have existed had another action been taken.

God knows all possible time lines. In determining which time line he will allow to be the real one, he considers the prayers that we offer.

In case you're now totally confused, let me try one more analogy: Twenty-eight-year-old Vladimir Kramnik from Russia is the greatest chess player in the world. He recently beat a computer named Deep Fritz that was programmed to consider all possible moves, up to more than twenty moves out. Can you fathom how many possible moves and counter-moves that is? But Kramnik beat the computer! That means he was able to picture each possible response the computer would give to his move, then each possible move he might make to each of those, then each possible move the computer would make to each of those possibilities, and so on, even better than the computer could.

Kramnik was impressed at least once, however, by the computer's genius. "I never imagined [the twenty-seventh move] and the tactics that followed," he said. "Only a computer would find and play something like that. I was completely shocked."[4] Kramnick was shocked by the *twenty-seventh* move. That's amazing to me, because when I play chess, I'm never able to plan past the twenty-sixth move! Truthfully, I usually can't even picture all my opponent's possibilities on the *next* move!

Now, if Vladimir Kramnik can consider every possibility in a game of chess, up to twenty-six moves away, don't you think the infinite, all-powerful, all-knowing God can consider all possible "moves" in this finite world he has created? What's more, God knows which move will be the *actual* one every time; and he moves accordingly, to make sure his will is accomplished. He allows us the freedom in this world to make moves and countermoves, and those decisions really matter to God. But God is never shocked, and he always wins.

C. S. Lewis explained how this principle applies to prayer:

> When we are praying the thought will often cross our minds that (if we only knew it) the event is already decided one way or the other. I believe this to be no good reason for ceasing our prayers, though the event certainly has been decided in a sense—it was decided "before all worlds." But one of the things that really caused it to happen may be this very prayer that we are now offering.[5]

The Bible says plainly that God changed his mind because of Moses' prayer. Moses' simple, heartfelt prayer—that you can read aloud in thirty seconds—dramatically changed the course of Jewish history.

PRAYER IS NOT DICTATION

Some people who accept that God can answer our prayers get the mistaken idea that prayer is therefore some kind of dictation to God. When they pray, they act as if they're telling God what to do, and he is supposed to do it. I heard a man say he was working to fix an electric light and couldn't get the lamp to work. He got frustrated, then said, "Lord, you made the electricity. You know more about it than I do. Fix it!" He flipped the switch, and it worked. I believe God can do anything (he created the light of the sun, so he can surely fix a lamp), but does he operate that way? Does he respond to a man's command to fix a lamp but not respond to a plea to heal a dying child or stop an out-of-control plane from crashing?

Each verse of God's Word should be taken in context with the rest of Scripture. When we study the Bible as a whole, we discover that prayer has some contingencies: We are to ask in Jesus' name (see John 14:13); we are to be in a state of obedience (see John 15:7); we must ask in faith (see James 1:5–7); we are to have the right motives (see James 4:3); and we are to ask "according to his will" (1 John 5:14).

God is not a genie to whom we go for hocus-pocus solutions. John Stott, author and former chaplain to the queen of England, said, "Prayer would place an impossible strain on every sensitive Christian, if he knew he was certain to get everything he asked for." Imagine the burden you would carry if every prayer you uttered was answered by God immediately! Imagine the ridiculous nature of our world if God granted every request. You would hate such a world. For our own good, we need to live in a world governed by certain basic scientific laws that are only interrupted on rare occasions, and then by a God who sees all, knows all, and cares about his children.

Yogi Berra was once catching in an important game for the Yankees. The score was tied in the bottom of the ninth inning. The pitcher crossed himself, then the batter stepped into the batter's box and crossed himself. Both were obviously seeking divine intervention for the next pitch to go their way. Yogi Berra quipped to the batter, "How about we just let God watch this one?"

It's impossible for God to give us everything we ask for. "Lord, help me strike him out," the pitcher might pray, while the batter is praying, "Lord, let me get a hit." Or, "Lord, we need rain for the crops," the farmer might pray, while the preacher says, "Lord, we need good weather for the church picnic."

My grandson Charlie is eight years old. He has two younger siblings—Tommy and Kimberly—who both are still in diapers and cry a lot. When he says his prayers before bed, Charlie often prays, "Please help Tommy and Kimberly to not cry their whole lives." I'm praying, "Lord, don't answer that prayer literally!" If Tommy gets hurt, I want him to be able to cry and let everybody know. If Kimberly is hungry, she only knows one way to tell her mom and dad—and that's to cry. And I hope when they get older they'll have soft hearts and be able to cry tears of joy and to weep at sad movies and shed tears of remorse when they sin.

But I don't worry about God answering that prayer. I know that God understands Charlie's immaturity and takes that into account. Don't you think the same is true for you and me? If God is all-powerful and all-knowing, and if God is a God of love, he's not going to give us everything we ask for. He will take into account our immaturity and limitations. No matter how much we think we know what's good for us, God sees the bigger picture and is interested in what is best for us. God's Word says, "In all things God works for the good of those who love him" (Romans 8:28).

When Jesus said, ask for whatever you want and it will be

given to you (see John 15:7), he knew people would understand the context—that God only gives us good gifts and that we, in our immaturity, sometimes don't know what to ask for; so we can trust that God, our loving Father, will give us what's best for us. Jesus himself was not a dictator in his prayers. In the Garden of Gethsemane he prayed, "Not my will, but yours be done" (Luke 22:42). Prayer is not meant to be dictation.

PRAYER IS NOT SIMPLY SUBMISSION

Others go to the opposite extreme and contend that God already has everything mapped out in advance, so prayer is simply meant to be submission of your personal will to his predetermined plan. These people pray, "Lord, if it is your will for my sick loved one to get well, help me to be grateful. If it is your will for her to die, help her—and me—to be ready." Or, "Lord, I'm without work. If it is in your plan that I find a job, help me to accept it and do my best at the job. If it is not in your plan, help me not to be resentful or envious."

Members of some denominations take this so far that if their child gets injured or sick, they'll pray for healing but refuse to go to the doctor out of an effort to be submissive to God's predetermined will. These people might say, "Who are we to dictate to God how his world is to be run? It's already predetermined—prayer is just getting in tune with God's will."

God does see and control the future, but at the same time, as we've discussed, we're not puppets on strings. The

Bible assures us that prayer changes things. God doesn't have everything about this world preprogrammed. God is sovereign, but that doesn't mean God rules over every detail to the extent that we are helpless. (If you believe God does have everything predestined, don't get upset with me. If it's true that God causes everything that happens, then he's causing me to disagree with you, so I must be within his will to say you are wrong!)

Some things are predetermined. The Bible makes it clear that God predetermined the time and place where you would live (see Acts 17:26), the plan for your redemption (see 1 Corinthians 2:7; Galatians 4:2–5; 2 Timothy 1:9), the time of Christ's return (see 2 Thessalonians 2:6), and many other significant events. But prayer can dramatically change a multitude of daily events and circumstances.

PRAYER IS COOPERATION WITH GOD

Instead of dictation or simple submission, prayer is our teaming up with God, joining our strength with his power. God operates this world by certain physical and spiritual laws. One of his spiritual laws is that his power is released through prayer. When we pray, we make it possible for his power to be released for our benefit. When we fail to pray, we limit God's blessing by our own weaknesses. James said, "You do not have, because you do not ask God" (James 4:2).

Pastor Tim Timmons said, "One of the deepest truths in life is that everything works better plugged in!" That doesn't mean God's power will be directed in exactly the way we dictate. But his power will flow through us to accomplish his will in a greater way.

In his book *The Prayer of Jabez*, Bruce Wilkinson tells about taking his preschooler, David, to the park. David watched some older children sliding down a huge slide and having a great time. Finally he mustered up the courage and began climbing that ladder. A third of the way up, he froze. One of the older kids yelled, "Get going!" But David was frozen with fear and couldn't go up or down. Wilkinson rushed over and hollered, "David, are you OK?" David, shaking and clinging to that ladder, asked his dad a predictable question: "Dad, will you go down the slide with me?"

Wilkinson called up to David, "Why, son?"

"I can't do it without you, Dad!" David called back, still trembling. "It's too big for me!"

Wilkinson says, "We climbed that long ladder up to the clouds together. At the top, I put my son between my legs and wrapped my arms around him. Then we went zipping down the slide together, laughing all the way."[6]

Prayer is saying, "Father, will you do this with me? I can't do it alone! It's too big for me!" Then, when you step out in faith, you discover that with your heavenly Father beside you, the sky's the limit!

WHY PRAYER MAKES A DIFFERENCE

Prayer changes God's mind because he loves us. God did not create us solely to be his servants. He created us to be his children. He wants a fatherly relationship with us, and he communicates as much when he allows us the power to change his mind.

A person's title can tell us a lot about him. If you asked me, "Who is Judy Russell?" I might say, "Well, she's been different things to me over the years. At first she was Good-Looking College Girl, then she was Friend, then Date, then Fiancée, then Wife. Now she is also Confidante, Lifelong Partner, and Boss!" All those titles help you understand who she is. There were a lot of names for God in the Old Testament, but Jesus introduced a revolutionary, more intimate concept of God. He said, "When you pray, say: 'Father'" (Luke 11:2).

We know God loves this name because it's the one Jesus used the most. More than two hundred times the gospel writers recorded Jesus' referring to God as "Father." In fact, the first recorded words of Jesus were, "Did you not know that I must be about My Father's business?" (Luke 2:49 NKJV). And his last words were, "Father, into your hands I commit my spirit" (Luke 23:46).

GOD IS A LOVING FATHER

Jesus wants you to understand that when you come to God with a need, you are petitioning a loving father. Let's say you are a father, and you plan a week's vacation for your family in the Smoky Mountains in Tennessee. You pile the kids in the car and head for Gatlinburg. If you were traveling from our city—Louisville, Kentucky—then you would probably think, *We'll make a pit stop at Berea, Kentucky. That's about a*

third of the way. Then we'll stop again just outside Knoxville,
Tennessee, to fill up with gas, and we'll eat lunch there. That
way we can get to Gatlinburg in about five hours.

Suppose you get a half-hour from home and your fourteen-
year-old son makes a request: "I've got some friends who are
going to Cancun for vacation. I don't want to go to the
Smoky Mountains," he whines. "Let's go to Cancun!" That
request is not going to be answered affirmatively no matter
how long he pleads or how hard he begs. Going to Cancun
is not in his best interest and probably not in your budget!
Someone said that God answers prayers one of four ways:
"Yes," "No," "Wait," and "You've gotta be kidding!" Some of
our prayer requests seem as silly to God as a fourteen-year-
old wanting to drive to Cancun. If we got what we asked for,
it would be detrimental to us. James 4:3 says, "When you ask,
you do not receive, because you ask with wrong motives, that
you may spend what you get on your pleasures."

But let's say that during your drive you get about an hour
down the road, and just outside Lexington, Kentucky, your
five-year-old says, "Daddy, I need to go to the bathroom."
You say, "We're going to stop in about a half-hour, if you can
wait." But he insists, "Dad, I really need to go to the bathroom." If you are a reasonable, loving father, you alter your
plans in favor of a reasonable request from the child you
love, whom you want to be happy and comfortable.

Jesus said in Matthew 7:7–11:

Ask and it will be given to you; seek and you will find;
knock and the door will be opened to you. For everyone

17

who asks receives; he who seeks finds; and to him who knocks, the door will be opened.

Which of you, if his son asks for bread, will give him a stone? Or if he asks for a fish, will give him a snake? If you, then, though you are evil, know how to give good gifts to your children, how much more will your Father in heaven give good gifts to those who ask him!

A key phrase in that passage is "good gifts." If your ten-year-old son asks for a boa constrictor for Christmas, you probably won't honor that request. You might give him a goldfish instead! God is giving from the perspective of a loving, wise parent who knows what's best in the long term.

Notice that Jesus didn't say, "Pray so that you can get in harmony with what God is going to do anyway." He said, "Pray and it will make a difference." God is like a loving father who enjoys responding to the requests of his children.

I like the title *Father* for God because I had a gentle, loving, patient, generous father. But maybe you didn't. The term *father* may conjure up a negative image for you. Let me tell you about two fathers who illustrate what Jesus meant when he said to refer to God as "Father."

A FATHER'S DEVOTION

Patrick Morley, in his book *The Man in the Mirror*, tells a heart-wrenching story about a father's love for his son. After spending the day salmon fishing in a secluded Alaskan bay, three men and a twelve-year-old boy got in a small seaplane to head home. Apparently one of the skis of the plane had

18

been punctured and had filled with water, causing the plane to crash shortly after takeoff. All four people survived the crash. After praying together, they abandoned the sinking plane and began to swim toward shore, fighting the cold waters and vicious riptide as they went. Two of the men, strong swimmers, reached the shore exhausted. The third man, the father of the twelve-year-old boy, saw that his son was unable to swim against the strong current. He swam back to his son.

The father tried desperately to save his son, but he couldn't pull his own weight and the boy's as well. Unable to pull his son to safety but unwilling to leave him, he cradled him in his arms as they were both swept out to sea. The father could have made it to shore by himself, but he loved his son too much to let him die alone.[6]

That's the kind of love and devotion our heavenly Father has for us. But the great news is that he didn't just die with us—he died for us. He died so that we could live. The Bible says: "God demonstrates his own love for us in this: While we were still sinners, Christ died for us" (Romans 5:8); "How great is the love the Father has lavished on us, that we should be called children of God!" (1 John 3:1); "Greater love has no one than this, that he lay down his life for his friends" (John 15:13).

A FATHER'S FORGIVENESS

There is another story that illustrates exactly what Jesus had in mind when he used the term *Father*. This is the story Jesus himself told (in Luke 15, paraphrased here) to describe the kind of God who is to be addressed as "Father":

> A certain man had two sons. The younger son said to his father, "Give me my share of the inheritance." The father gave him a generous advance on his half of the inheritance. The boy left home and wasted his wealth in a wild party life. He was soon penniless and friendless, and he took a job with a farmer, feeding pigs. He got so hungry at times that he was tempted to eat the slop that those unclean animals were being fed.
>
> Finally one day he came to his senses and asked, "What's wrong with me? My father's servants are treated better than this. I'll humble myself and go to my father and admit that I've sinned. I'll ask him to take me in as one of his servants. At least then I'll have enough to eat."
>
> The young man headed toward home. As he walked down that long road, the question that dominated his thinking was, *How will my father react when he sees me?* The son played out several scenarios in his mind as he traveled. *Worst-case scenario,* he thought, *is he refuses to see me. Best case…well, probably the best I can hope for is that I talk him into giving me a chance as a servant.*

But what kind of father did he have? Jesus said the father saw his son from a long way off. He had been watching for him. The child may have been out of the father's house, but he was never out of the father's heart. The father was a man of unconditional love—he ran to meet his son. He was a father who was anxious to forgive—he smothered his son's repentant speech against his shoulder and called out, "Bring out some decent clothes for this boy and some new shoes for his feet! Go tell the chef to butcher the best we've got, and let's have a feast! My son was dead, but he's alive again; he was lost, but now he is found! He's home, he's hungry, and I'm happy. Let's celebrate!"

HEAVEN STOPS AS THE FATHER LISTENS

That's the kind of father Jesus wants you to picture when you pray, "Our Father." The Bible says, "You did not receive a spirit that makes you a slave again to fear, but you received the Spirit of sonship. And by him we cry, 'Abba, Father.' The Spirit himself testifies with our spirit that we are God's children" (Romans 8:15–16). *Abba* is an intimate term in Aramaic; in English, we would say, "Daddy." God answers your prayers because he loves you as a good father loves his children.

As our church has grown larger and my responsibilities have increased, I've been forced to learn how to protect my time. Otherwise I would spend all of my time answering the phone and conducting impromptu counseling sessions, and the scope of our ministry would be much smaller. But there have always been two people besides my wife who have permission to walk into my office at any time. They also have my inner-office phone number and can call me at any moment. If they need me, I stop whatever I'm doing and talk to them. It doesn't matter how important the meeting or study might be, I will stop and give attention for one reason: They are my sons. I love them more than anyone else.

The Bible says that when you submit your life to God through his Son, Jesus, you are adopted into his family. You are a child of God, and you can have his attention at any moment. He invites you to pray and promises he will listen. And when you do call out to him, "Abba, Father!" he comes running.

Max Lucado wrote:

> You can talk to God because God listens. Your voice matters in heaven. He takes you very seriously. When you enter his presence, the attendants turn to you to hear your voice. No need to fear that you will be ignored. Even if you stammer or stumble, even if what you have to say impresses no one, it impresses God—and he listens. He listens to the painful plea of the elderly in the rest home. He listens to the gruff confession of the death-row inmate. When the alcoholic begs for mercy, when the spouse seeks guidance, when the businessman steps off the street into the chapel, God listens.
>
> Intently. Carefully. The prayers are honored as precious jewels. Purified and empowered, the words rise in a delightful fragrance to our Lord. "The smoke from the incense went up from the angel's hand to God" (Rev. 8:4). Incredible. Your words do not stop until they reach the very throne of God.
>
> One call and heaven's fleet appears. Your prayer on earth activates God's power in heaven.
>
> You are the "someone" of God's kingdom. Your prayers move God to change the world. You may not understand the mystery of prayer. You don't need to. But this much is clear: Actions in heaven begin when someone prays on earth. What an amazing thought!
>
> When you speak, Jesus hears.
>
> And when Jesus hears, the world is changed.
>
> All because someone prayed.[7]

Chapter Two

GOD STILL ANSWERS PRAYER

When I pray, coincidences happen.
When I don't pray, coincidences don't happen.
—Bishop William Temple

I'm convinced that God still answers prayer today. Several scientific studies have verified the benefit of prayer. For example, the September 2001 issue of the *Journal of Reproductive Health* reported on a study out of Columbia University School of Medicine on the power of prayer. They studied women battling infertility and discovered that their likelihood of conceiving doubled when people—even total strangers—prayed for them. Another study found that people undergoing risky cardiovascular surgery had fewer complications when they were the focus of prayer groups.[1] But I don't need independent, double-blind studies to prove to me that God answers prayer, because I've witnessed it myself. The following stories are from personal experience.

A MOTHER'S PRAYER

I know I'm a preacher today because of my mother's prayers. When I was born, my mother began praying that I would become a minister. She also did her part. She planted the idea in my mind when I was very young. She would occasionally hug me and whisper in my ear, "You'd make a good preacher someday."

When I became a teenager, my mother never mentioned the ministry to me. Years later I asked her why she didn't say anything to me in my teen years about entering the ministry. She said wisely, "That was the wrong time to mention it. I knew at that age you'd want to do just the opposite of what I wanted you to do!" But she continued to mention the idea to God in her daily prayers.

During my adolescence, being a preacher was the furthest thing from my mind. It wasn't cool to say you were going into the ministry, and I wanted to be popular. Also, I grew up in a small church where I wasn't exposed to many great ministry role models; so my opinion of preachers wasn't very high. I was into sports, and I thought I wanted to become a high school basketball or football coach.

But the primary reason I didn't want to preach was that getting up in front of people terrified me! I hated public speaking. I even trembled when I had to read aloud in front of the class.

During my last two years of high school, I gave my mother a lot of gray hair. I'm sure at times, rather than praying I'd be a preacher, she just prayed I would be a Christian! But in April of my senior year, I had a change of heart. My dad took me to visit a secular college I thought I wanted to attend in the fall. On the way home, as I reflected on the visit, I told my dad I knew that wasn't where I was supposed to go. I came home and told my mother that I had decided to go to Cincinnati Bible College and study for the ministry. The announcement was unexpected, and my mother wept, which she didn't do very often. At the time I didn't understand why. I didn't know she'd been praying for so long that I would enter the ministry. I've since come to understand why I felt the way I did on that trip home. I was moved to enter the ministry because God still answers prayer.

SURVIVING CANCER

When I was a senior in college, I got a letter from my mother explaining that she had discovered a lump in her breast and was going to have it removed. In the days that followed, I learned to pray at a new level of intensity. I pleaded with God for the tumor to be benign.

On the day of the surgery, I paced the floor of the dorm, waiting for the call from my sister back home, four hundred miles away. When she called, the news was not good: "It's malignant," she said. "It's reached some of the lymph nodes. She'll have a complete mastectomy. All the lymph nodes and muscles will be removed. She'll have to go through thirty days of radiation after that."

I learned that God doesn't always answer our prayers the way we want him to, even when we pray with intensity. But our family and close friends determined to keep on praying for healing. We prayed every day. My mother is now eighty-six years old, and the cancer has never recurred. God still answers prayer.

THIRTY MILLION DOLLARS

In 1993 our church prayed fervently that God would help us raise $26 million to build a new church building. That was $26 million over our regular budget, to be raised over a period of three years, and double our offerings at the time. It was one of the largest financial campaigns a church had ever attempted. Financial experts told us it was impossible.

We didn't tell people in the church what amount to give. We just asked them to pray about what God would have them do. When the day came, we received nearly $31 million in commitments! In a four-year period we collected more than $40 million. That was an incredible answer to prayer. Financial experts insisted it was a miracle.

Ten years later, in 2003, we again needed to expand. We set a goal of raising $30 million. The task seemed daunting. The economy was down, and the country was on the brink of war. The need for classroom space was paramount but not highly visible to most of our members. And a large percentage of our congregation is made up of new Christians. Other organizations were struggling to raise funds. But we felt led by God to go forward, and we prayed that he would bless our efforts. Only he could move in the hearts of enough people to give enough money to meet the goal. If it happened, it would be because God was in it.

On the day we announced the total commitments to

give, I was as stunned as anyone—our congregation had committed to give more than $35 million! More than six thousand families had promised to contribute. Not one gift was over a half-million dollars. The median gifts were in the $10,000 to $25,000 range. If you know anything about fund-raising, you know that to get so many people committed to one cause is evidence that God still answers prayer!

BRETT DEYOUNG'S BRAIN TUMOR

Brett DeYoung has been on our staff for ten years. He's a key administrator in our church. He's forty-six years old, a cyclist, an outdoorsman, and a picture of good health. But in September 2002, just a few weeks before I was scheduled to preach on this topic of answered prayer, he had a seizure at church and was rushed to the hospital. In the ambulance, he suffered a second grand mal seizure.

An MRI revealed that Brett had a brain tumor. The whole church body was asked to pray for him. Our staff held a twenty-four-hour prayer vigil. Brett underwent surgery.

The news was not good. Brett's tumor was rare and difficult to operate on. Surgeons couldn't determine exactly where the tumor ended and brain tissue began. Instead of removing the tumor, they had been forced to take a few biopsies, staple Brett's skull back together, and do further study. The doctors believed the tumor was malignant—a stage-two cancer. They hoped a second surgery would allow them to remove 90 percent of the tumor. Brett would have to undergo radiation treatment or chemotherapy to try to take care of the rest.

The church staff held a second twenty-four-hour prayer vigil. The church body prayed. We discovered that people all over the country and, literally, all over the world, were praying for Brett DeYoung.

The results of the second surgery were spectacular. The doctors were able to remove the entire tumor; no treatment would be necessary. Brett's faculties were unaffected. Just two weeks later, Brett was able to attend our staff meeting! When he walked to the front of the chapel where our staff of three hundred had gathered, they stood and cheered. Brett thanked them for their prayers. We celebrated and thanked God for his answers.

God still answers prayer!

SEARCHING FOR A THIRD PREACHER

The leaders of our church felt led to hire a third man for our preaching team at Southeast. I am almost sixty years old and nearing retirement. Dave Stone, our second preacher, is now in his forties. We wanted to add a third, younger person to share the preaching load and appeal to the younger members of our church. We prayed and combed the country for three years looking for the right person. We were looking for someone in his late twenties or early thirties, a man of integrity, giftedness, and maturity beyond his years.

Then, at the North American Christian Convention in

the summer of 2002, Dave and I heard Kyle Idleman speak. He was the youngest preacher ever invited to speak to the convention. We already knew Kyle well. He had been an intern in our preaching department just a few years earlier, and everyone who worked with him loved him. His dad serves as the president of Ozark Christian College, and Dave and I have known the family for years.

Kyle's name had come up before as a possible candidate for the third preacher. At first we thought he was too inexperienced. Then, a couple of years later, we didn't think he would be interested in the position—he already had a successful ministry in southern California. In just three years, the church Kyle had helped plant was running more than one thousand in attendance, and things were going well for him. After we heard him preach at the convention, though, Dave and I were convinced that Kyle was the man for the job. We decided that we had to ask him even though, to be honest, we didn't think there was much chance of his saying yes.

But the Bible says, "You have not because you ask not"; so we prayed, and I contacted Kyle. To our delight, Kyle said he would consider the position because of his admiration for our church. He agreed to come to Louisville with his wife for an exploratory visit.

Our church elders had seen a video of one of Kyle's sermons and really liked him, but they insisted that they weren't ready to make a decision without going through the proper procedures. Other candidates should be considered, and a few elders should probably fly to California to observe Kyle's ministry there. Since we don't usually hold elders' meetings in the summer, this process would normally be delayed until later in the year. But our chairman had insisted that we meet that particular season and had set the dates sometime earlier. So when Kyle, unaware of these inner workings, announced the dates he would be coming to visit, we were intrigued to learn that they would coincide with our meeting. Kyle agreed to join us.

The Holy Spirit specially anointed that elders' meeting. Kyle came with such a humble and sincere spirit that their hearts melted. When he left, everyone agreed: Kyle was our man. This is the right thing. God has answered our prayers. They were so excited that one elder suggested, "Let's send a committee over to the hotel right now and tell him we're unanimous—we want him to come, and we want to give him a tangible offer."

In the meantime, Kyle had returned to his hotel room and told his wife, Desiree, "I think the Holy Spirit really worked in that meeting. I felt good about it, but I just wish there was some confirmation that they felt the same way and that this is really what the Lord wants us to do." Within minutes the phone rang; several of our elders were in the hotel lobby and wanted to speak with Kyle right away!

Kyle accepted our offer to join the preaching team, and in spite of an economic recession, the Idlemans' California home sold in three days. Desiree searched the Internet for a house in Kentucky. She found one she liked, and Kyle came to settle the purchase. In October 2002, he preached his first sermon at Southeast, and the congregation fell in love with him.

For three years we had prayed for a third man and received no answer. Then, in three months, the man was found, arrangements were made, and a new ministry was started. God still answers prayer!

HOW GOD USUALLY ANSWERS PRAYER

You're probably thinking, *What about the prayers that aren't answered? What about the guy who died of a brain tumor? What about the mother who prayed for her child, but he turned against the Lord? What about the church that's been praying for a pastor and can't find one?*

The list of unanswered prayers seems endless. A man met me in the hallway when he heard I would be preaching about answered prayer. He said, "I have a question I hope you'll answer. My wife prayed every day that the Lord would take away her depression. He never did. She took her own life because she couldn't get over the hump. Why didn't he answer her prayer?"

I've prayed for an empty church building to sell, and it didn't. I've prayed for financial burdens to be lifted, and they weren't. I've prayed for people to respond to the gospel, and they never have. Why is that?

This book has three parts: God Answers Prayer; God Answers Prayer *Dramatically;* and God Answers Prayer Dramatically, *but Not Always.* We'll discuss the "not always" part in the last section and seek to answer that question. But in the meantime, here's the most important lesson for part 1 of this book: *God often answers prayer in nondramatic, non-miraculous ways.*

THE DIFFERENCE BETWEEN MIRACLES AND ANSWERED PRAYER

Not every answered prayer is a miracle. Dr. Norman Geisler, in his book *Miracles and Modern Thought,* defined a miracle as "a divine intervention into, or an interruption of, the regular course of the world."[2] C. S. Lewis defined a miracle as "an interference with Nature by supernatural power."[3] I like those definitions.

Some people call every intervention of God a miracle. If God impresses an idea on the mind or gives someone a safe trip in heavy traffic, they say it's a miracle. But a miracle in the Bible was a physical manifestation of God so visible, so supernatural, and so impressive that it was undeniable. Even Jesus' enemies couldn't deny that a miracle had been performed. They tried to say that his power must be satanic, but they couldn't deny what had been done.[4] When God decided to listen to Moses' prayer and spare the Israelites, that was answered prayer; but it wouldn't be classified as a miracle, because no one witnessed anything supernatural.

It's important to make this distinction. If you call every answered prayer a miracle, you lessen the significance and meaning of the word *miracle.* You also risk undermining your testimony to the world. If it rains and you say, "That's a miracle!" someone will raise an eyebrow and say, "No, that's the aftermath of the hurricane that just hit the coast of Florida." However, if you say, "I've been praying for rain, and I'm so thankful it came," you don't lose credibility.

Take for example the story of Brett DeYoung's surgery. The doctors said, "We've removed a tumor the size of a prune, and we have good news. We think we got it all, and follow-up radiation won't be necessary." We should give God thanks for answered prayer. Did God intervene? We believe he did. Can we call it a miracle? Technically, no, because no one witnessed a supernatural event. If the doctors had opened Brett's skull and discovered that the tumor they had seen in the previous surgery was no longer there, that would be an act of God contrary to the laws of nature. If we say the successful surgery was a miracle, we may lose credibility with the surgeons and attending physicians who might respond, "We've removed those kinds of tumors before."

Here's an interesting side note: After I expressed some of these thoughts in a sermon, saying that we should call Brett's successful surgery answered prayer but not a miracle, I was contacted by two doctors. One suggested that I should be careful about too quickly calling something an answer to prayer. He was concerned about the implications if Brett's tumor were to return. The other doctor said I should have classified Brett's experience a miracle because an entire series of events had to take place which were beyond human explanation in order for things to transpire the way they did. How about that—a doctor trying to convince the preacher that what happened was a miracle!

Whether Brett's surgery was a miracle or not depends largely on how you define *miracle*. If every intervention of God is a miracle, then every answered prayer is a miracle. If we pray for rain and it rains, if we pray for our child's health and he or she recovers from an illness, if we get the promotion we prayed for, we can classify each of those as a miracle. But I think it weakens the significance of the supernatural acts of God that have occurred only rarely in history if we call every answered prayer a miracle. Even in biblical times, hundreds of years passed between supernatural events. Most people lived their whole lives without ever witnessing a miracle. That's why I prefer defining a miracle as a visible act of God (or his agent) that supersedes the normal laws of nature.

When the sun stands still, when the mouths of hungry lions are shut, when a blind man suddenly sees, when the deaf hear, when a withered hand is restored, when the dead are raised—those are miracles. A miracle is a visible, undeniable act of God that appears to contradict the laws of nature. God is capable of performing these things, and at times God has intervened in visible ways. But such events are not commonplace. Most of the time, when God intervenes, he does so quietly and anonymously—in such a way that we must accept by faith that he has answered our prayers.

GIVING GOD CREDIT

Before the Persian Gulf War in 1991, I saw a sign over a fast-food restaurant that read, "Pray for America." After the impressive victory, the same sign read, "Way to go, troops!" Was the Desert Storm victory a miracle? No. Was it an answer to prayer? Yes. It was certainly appropriate to congratulate the troops, but even more importantly, we need to give God credit for answering our prayers.

My brother, John Russell, who preaches at the Lakeside Christian Church in Northern Kentucky, told a story about a poor widow who was always thanking God for her blessings. Her next-door neighbor was an atheist who grew tired of her spiritual talk. One day he overheard her praying, "God, I have nothing to feed my children today. Please provide our daily bread."

The atheist thought he'd teach the lady a lesson. He bought several bags of groceries, sat them on the front porch, rang the doorbell, and hid. The widow came out, saw the groceries, and burst into praise. "Thank you, God! You have supplied my need! Thank you for answering my prayer! 'Bless the Lord, O my soul!'"

The atheist stepped out from behind a bush and arrogantly said, "Ma'am, God hasn't supplied your need today— I did! See how foolish it is to trust in a nonexistent God and give him credit for what he didn't do?"

The woman paused, then burst into another prayer: "Dear God, you are so wonderful! You not only provided food for me today, you got the devil to pay for it!"

God often answers prayer through nonmiraculous means. But it's still answered prayer, and he ought to get the glory.

WHEN GOD ANSWERED MY PRAYER

In 1997 I traveled deep into the heart of India on a mission trip. Our trip was nearing an end when I began to have some pain in my leg. Half-jokingly, I said to the two doctors who were traveling with me, "I've got a pain in the back of my calf. I think I've got phlebitis!"

Both the doctors were poker-faced, but I later learned that when I was out of earshot, one of them said to the other, "What would we do if we were faced with a case of deep-vein thrombosis out here?"

"I don't even want to think about it!" the other responded. They had brought a lot of medical supplies, but nothing to treat that kind of condition.

Several hours later, when Dr. David Dageforde saw me limping, he said, "Let me take a look at that leg." He took one look at the swelling and became very somber. Dr. Dageforde rarely gets rattled, so I knew something was seriously wrong. "Folks," he said, "we have a serious problem here. If this man were in the United States, I'd hospitalize him and immobilize him for a week. We must head back to town immediately so we can get proper medicine."

The problem was, we were about as far from civilization as we could be—it was a six-hour drive to the closest town, Damoh, where the doctors hoped some heparin (a blood thinner) might be available. The nearest hospital—in Delhi—was an additional twelve-hour train ride away!

Within twenty minutes, some team members placed me in a car with two pillows under my leg, and we headed for

Damoh. When I say the trip was wild, you can't imagine what I mean unless you've been to a Third-World country. We drove at what felt like breakneck speed, but the roads were in such rough condition that it took six hours to travel 150 miles. Indian roads are filled not only with cars but with pedestrians, bicyclists, oxcarts, farm animals, and a multitude of large trucks and buses. Drivers play chicken with oncoming vehicles, waiting until the last second before veering off to avoid a collision.

Though I knew my life was in danger, I felt no fear. I have always preached that if you encounter a trial, the Lord will sustain you. And this certainly qualified as a trial. I was faced with hours of uncertainty—not knowing what the odds were that a blood clot would move into my heart or lungs and cause serious problems or even death. Were the chances that I would lose my life 1 percent? Two percent? Higher? I didn't know; but I wasn't afraid. I don't know whether God was answering my own prayers or those of dozens of people who had committed to praying for me during the two weeks I was gone, but I know that when I needed him most, God was there to bolster my faith and courage.

The farther we drove, the more I reasoned that my chances of dying from a blood clot had to be a lot lower than the odds of being killed in an accident driving at night on those roads! We passed many vehicles with no lights, no warning at all of their approach.

I also reasoned that the entire event was too bizarre to be coincidental. I was in the most remote area I had ever traveled to, and suddenly I was experiencing the only serious health threat I had ever encountered. I knew that God must have some reason for allowing the crisis, if only to teach me to rely more completely on him.

Though it was comforting to know that I was with two doctors who were experts in their fields, the source of my peace was in knowing that I was exactly where God wanted me to be. The safest place in the world to be is in the will of God, and many things had happened during those two weeks to confirm that I was in the right place.

The Bible says, "Trust in the LORD with all your heart and lean not on your own understanding; in all your ways acknowledge him, and he will make your paths straight" (Proverbs 3:5–6). I didn't know for certain that I was going to be OK, but I did know that what was happening had a purpose, and God was with me. I was so calm that I joked about the multimillion-dollar keyman insurance policy the bank made the church take out on me when we applied for such a large loan for the new facilities. "If I die," I said, "next Sunday Dave Stone will announce, 'We have some bad news and some good news. The bad news is that Bob Russell died this week. The good news is that the building is paid for!'"

We finally arrived in Damoh and were able to obtain some heparin. Dr. Russ Summay started an IV, and I was confined to bed. We began drawing up a strategy for the next leg of the trip to Delhi, where my leg could be x-rayed. Assuming that all went well, we could probably catch our scheduled flight home to Louisville in four days. "The one

38

thing I don't want to do," I insisted, "is wind up staying in a hospital in India."

A few weeks earlier, at the end of the Southeast New Year's Eve service, a church member had approached me with his business card. He introduced himself as Dave Graves and told me he had been working for General Electric in New Delhi since June. "If there's anything Karen [his wife] and I can do for you while you're in India, please call us—here's my card."

I get a lot of business cards and don't keep all of them, but I put Dave's in my wallet, not knowing that even in that small gesture, God was watching out for me.

Now, after a lengthy train ride to Delhi, I called Dave for some help in my time of need. He recommended a medical clinic where the American ambassador goes for treatment, so I was taken to the small, thirty-bed hospital in a nice section of town.

The Indian doctor examined me and reported exactly what I did not want to hear: "It's too dangerous to get on a plane in this condition. The air pressure could dislodge the clot. You need to stay here in the hospital for the next five days."

I protested, but I realized I had no choice. I was admitted to the hospital. There I was, doing precisely what I had said I didn't want to do. But God took care of me. The hospital wasn't elaborate—probably the equivalent of a 1950s hospital in America—but I received excellent treatment. I was placed in a private room where two nurses took turns caring for me, actually sitting with me for twelve-hour shifts. They were stuck listening to me talk about Christianity for hours!

My longtime friends Russ and Jane Summay elected to stay in Delhi while the other team members returned to Louisville. Dave and Karen Graves and another couple from our church, Vern and Barb Fleming, who also happened to be in India, stopped by to visit and brought me food. I had a phone in my room and was able to receive calls from family and friends back home.

After four days the swelling had gone down, and the major risks were eliminated. But now, with visitors gone, a strange feeling came over me. For the first time since the ordeal had begun, I was afraid. *What if I have to have surgery here? I'm all alone. I can't speak the language. That would be terrible!* My heart started to pound, I became short of breath, and I felt as though my lungs were collapsing.

Then another thought occurred to me: *Why am I suddenly afraid? The danger is nearly over. Other travelers have gone through worse than this; what's wrong with me?* I still had my laptop computer and my Bible software with me, so I began to look up scriptures about fear:

> The LORD is my light and my salvation—whom shall I fear? The LORD is the stronghold of my life—of whom shall I be afraid. (Psalm 27:1)

> Do not fear, for I am with you; do not be dismayed, for I am your God. I will strengthen you and help you; I will uphold you with my righteous right hand. (Isaiah 41:10)

God did not give us a spirit of timidity, but a spirit of power, of love and of self-discipline. (2 Timothy 1:7)

Do not let your hearts be troubled. Trust in God; trust also in me. (John 14:1)

Next I started to sing: "Jesus, You're My Firm Foundation..."; "In Christ Alone..."; even songs from my childhood, like, "Come into My Heart, Lord, Jesus." I'm sure if you had walked into the hospital room at that moment, you would have been anything but inspired. It was not a pretty sound!

Just then the nurse came to take my blood pressure, as she did regularly. My pressure had always been normal, but not so this time. "A little hypertension?" she asked. No way, I thought. Not me! But the fear had actually made my blood pressure rise. The nurse left, and I resumed my singing. Finally I settled down, and my pressure returned to normal. But I was still puzzled at why I had suddenly become so afraid.

That evening I reflected on the story in Acts 12 of Peter's being escorted out of prison by an angel as the church was praying for him. The Bible says the angel went with him for a block and then left. Suddenly Peter was on his own—by himself, in the middle of a dangerous city, in the middle of the night. He had been freed—the worst danger was behind him—but now he was alone. Had he felt afraid?

Then it started to make sense. God does for you what you can't do for yourself. Because of prayer—my own and scores of others—I was lifted up in a pressure situation. It wasn't until the danger had passed that I had been released to walk the rest of the journey on my own. That realization comforted me in a dark and lonely hospital room halfway around the world. In my time of greatest need, God had been faithful. He came in a nondramatic, nonmiraculous way—but God answered my prayer.

Chapter Three

THE KIND OF PRAYER GOD ANSWERS

Prayer does not fit us for the greater works;
prayer is the greater work.

—Oswald Chambers, *My Utmost for His Highest*

I read about a small Kentucky town that had two churches and one distillery. Members of both churches complained that the distillery gave the community a bad image. To make matters worse, the owner of the distillery was an outspoken atheist.

The two churches decided to hold a joint Saturday-night prayer meeting to ask God to intervene and settle the matter once and for all. The church folks gathered on the designated evening and began to pray.

All through the prayer meeting, a terrible electric storm raged. To the delight of the church members, lightning struck that old distillery and burned it to the ground. The next morning, the sermon in both churches was on the power of prayer.

Insurance adjusters promptly notified the distillery that they wouldn't pay for the damages. The fire was caused by an "act of God," and that was an exclusion in their policy.

The distillery owner was furious. He decided to sue both churches, claiming they had conspired with God to destroy his building and business. The churches denied they had anything to do with the cause of the fire.

The judge in the case opened the trial with these words: "I find one thing in this case most perplexing: We have a situation here where the plaintiff, an atheist, is professing his belief in the power of prayer, and the defendants, all faithful church members, are denying the very same power!"

Most of us wouldn't deny that there is power in prayer. A recent survey found that 76 percent of Americans say they pray, and more than 50 percent pray every day. When American Christians were asked what subjects they wanted to hear about when they went to church, the number one request was, "How to make prayer more effective." The hottest-selling Christian book for the last several years has been *The Prayer of Jabez* by Bruce Wilkinson. It's just ninety-two pages and is based on the daring prayer of an obscure man in the Old Testament. It has sold several million copies and has made the *New York Times* bestseller list. Why is it so popular? I'm sure there are several reasons, but one is that people sense there is a power in prayer and that they haven't fully tapped into that power.

James talks about prayer that is "powerful and effective" (James 5:16). The Greek word for *effective* is the word from which we get our term *energy*. Prayer can energize your life, but the Bible makes it clear there are certain conditions that must be met first.

PRAYER IN JESUS' NAME

James says that a prerequisite to powerful prayers is that they be "in the name of the Lord" (James 5:14). Jesus said, "The Father will give you whatever you ask in my name" (John 15:16). There is power in the name of Jesus. But that doesn't mean Jesus' name can be used as some kind of magical incantation. There is power in the name of Jesus because of what is being communicated when you pray "in Jesus' name."

WHICH GOD YOU'RE CALLING

When you say at the end of your prayer, "In Jesus' name," you are defining which God you're praying to. You are not praying to Baal, Allah, Buddha, or some pantheistic force. You're praying to the God who manifested himself in Jesus Christ. Christians believe in the God who made himself known in Jesus. That's not the same god to whom people of other religions pray. The power of prayer comes in praying to the one true God, the one who was incarnate in Jesus and who commanded us to pray in the name of his Son.

A few years ago I was asked to pray at a civic event. When I arrived, the person who had invited me said tactfully, "Please remember that there are a variety of religions represented." It was a veiled request not to pray in Jesus' name, because not everyone present was a Christian. But I didn't feel right not praying in Jesus' name. What should I do? I decided to end the prayer, "in the name of the Lion of Judah." After I prayed, I thought to myself, *I'm so clever.*

That was shrewd. I prayed in Jesus' name, because Jesus is the Lion of Judah, but I didn't offend anybody. How smart I am!

Then I was convicted. I thought, *That wasn't shrewd—it was cowardly.* Jesus said, "*If you are ashamed of me and my words, I will be ashamed of you.*" I decided that from that time forward, I would pray unashamedly in the name of Jesus. If people don't want me to pray in Jesus' name, they shouldn't ask me.

More recently, I was asked to pray at another civic event, and I offered the prayer in Jesus' name. A young lady approached me afterward and said, "I was offended that you prayed in Jesus' name." She was dignified and pleasant, and I wanted her to like me. But I knew I shouldn't apologize for what I did. I said, "I'm sorry you were offended, but if Jesus is Lord of my life, I have to pray in Jesus' name. He commanded me to pray in his name, and he's more important to me than whether I offend someone." I told her I hoped she understood. I'm not sure she did, but whether she did or not doesn't really matter. I have to be obedient whether people understand or not, and whether people like me or not.

THE KINGDOM WHERE YOU BELONG

When you pray in Jesus' name, you're also communicating to God that you acknowledge the authority of Jesus in your life. You might begin an appeal to the governor of your state by saying, "Mr. Governor, I've been a citizen of this state all my life." Your appeal won't carry nearly as much weight if you don't live in his state. When Paul appealed to Caesar, he did so as a Roman citizen. When you pray in Jesus' name, you're saying, "God, I'm coming to you as a citizen of your kingdom. I'm a follower of Christ. I'm one of your children."

WHO YOUR MEDIATOR IS

The Bible says, "There is one God and one mediator between God and men, the man Christ Jesus" (1 Timothy 2:5). When you pray in Jesus' name, you're calling on Christ and his Holy Spirit to mediate between you and God. Paul promised:

> The Spirit helps us in our weakness. We do not know what we ought to pray for, but the Spirit himself intercedes for us with groans that words cannot express. And he who searches our hearts knows the mind of the Spirit, because the Spirit intercedes for the saints in accordance with God's will. (Romans 8:26–27)

What a promise! Haven't you ever felt like you didn't really know what to pray for? When you pray in Jesus' name, the Holy Spirit intercedes for you. He knows you better than you know yourself. He also knows the will of God because he is one with God. Only the Spirit of God can bring your heart and God's heart together to make something happen that is agreeable to both parties.

PRAYER ACCORDING TO GOD'S WILL

We usually end our prayers with, "In Jesus' name, amen." The word *amen* simply means "so be it." We're saying, "In Jesus' name, may it be so." When you pray in the name of the Lord, you're submitting your will to his will. You're

47

acknowledging that if both parties don't agree, you want God's will to prevail. You're saying, "May it be so, Lord, as long as this prayer is in accordance with the name, the will, and the character of your Son, Jesus Christ."

We don't dictate to God what he is supposed to do. As Jesus himself prayed in Gethsemane, so we should pray: "Not my will but yours be done." For instance, instead of begging God to heal someone we love, we should pray, "Lord, we desire this person to be healed. He or she wants to get better. We join our voices in asking for healing. We ask for your power to flow and to bring this person to health. But we also have a spirit of surrender to your will. We want you to accomplish your purpose in us. In Jesus' name, amen."

PRAYER OF FAITH

Jesus said, "If you have faith as small as a mustard seed, you can say to this mountain, 'Move from here to there' and it will move. Nothing will be impossible for you" (Matthew 17:20). The Bible says, "The prayer offered in faith will make the sick person well" (James 5:15). If you want God to answer your prayer, begin with the confidence that there is a God who created you, loves you, and wants to respond to your prayer.

It only makes sense that faith would be a prerequisite to answered prayer. If you don't believe God can answer your prayer, either you're not going to offer the prayer at all, or you're going to offer a halfhearted, hypocritical prayer. God cannot be mocked. He knows your heart. If you offer a prayer that's more like an incantation or an effort to cover all your bases just in case someone is up there listening, a righteous and holy God is not going to encourage such pretense by answering the prayer.

In another passage, James said of the praying person, "When he asks, he must believe and not doubt, because he who doubts is like a wave of the sea, blown and tossed by the wind. That man should not think he will receive anything from the Lord; he is a double-minded man, unstable in all he does" (James 1:6–8).

Does that mean if you have any doubts, your prayer won't be answered? No. A man once asked Jesus to heal his demon-possessed son. The Bible says:

> When the spirit saw Jesus, it immediately threw the boy into a convulsion. He fell to the ground and rolled around, foaming at the mouth.
> Jesus asked the boy's father, "How long has he been like this?"
> "From childhood," he answered. "It has often thrown him into fire or water to kill him. But if you can do anything, take pity on us and help us."
> "'If you can'?" said Jesus. "Everything is possible for him who believes."
> Immediately the boy's father exclaimed, "I do believe; help me overcome my unbelief!" (Mark 9:20–24)

Jesus didn't refuse to help the man because he had doubts. Jesus commanded the spirit to leave the boy, and from that point on, the boy was healed.

Everyone has doubts. God doesn't expect perfect faith,

but he does expect sincere faith. God wants you to come to him with a genuine heart, believing that he is good and has the power to answer your prayer. You may have to say, "I believe; help my unbelief!" But you must be earnestly reaching out to God in faith, lest you offend the Creator with a halfhearted, patronizing prayer sent into the air "in case someone's up there." The Bible says, "Without faith it is impossible to please God, because anyone who comes to him must believe that he exists and that he rewards those who earnestly seek him" (Hebrews 11:6).

PRAYER OF A RIGHTEOUS PERSON

The Bible says, "Confess your sins to each other and pray for each other so that you may be healed. The prayer of a righteous man is powerful and effective" (James 5:16). The person more likely to see answers to his prayers is the righteous person—one who has a right relationship with God and with others.

RIGHT RELATIONSHIP WITH OTHERS

By commanding that we confess our sins to one another, James insinuates that a person who wants God to hear his prayers must be in a right relationship with others. The Bible makes it clear that we cannot have a right relationship with God if we're full of hatred for our brother or sister:

> If anyone says, "I love God," yet hates his brother, he is a liar. For anyone who does not love his brother, whom

50

he has seen, cannot love God, whom he has not seen. And he has given us this command: Whoever loves God must also love his brother. (1 John 4:20–21)

A loving parent wants his children to get along with one another. Before God grants credibility to your prayers, he wants you to be in harmony with your Christian brothers and sisters. Jesus commanded:

> If you are offering your gift at the altar and there remember that your brother has something against you, leave your gift there in front of the altar. First go and be reconciled to your brother; then come and offer your gift. (Matthew 5:23–24)

When you are at odds with another Christian, you are at odds with God, and you are not ready to pray. Go make things right with your brother, then offer your prayer to God.

Let me add a word of caution about this command to confess your sins: Confessing your sins doesn't mean spilling your guts to everyone or airing your dirty laundry in public. Years ago a young, unmarried couple came forward at the end of a service and asked permission to speak to the congregation. We used to immediately introduce anyone who came forward, so I introduced them and told the congregation they had something to say. "We want to confess that we have committed fornication," they announced. "We want to ask your forgiveness." How awkward! Few people even knew them, and none of us had been aware of their sin.

People responded kindly, but it was an uncomfortable moment!

Warren Wiersbe offered words of wisdom:

We must never confess sin beyond the circle of that sin's influence. Private sin requires private confession; public sin requires public confession. It is wrong for Christians to hang dirty wash in public, for such confessing might do more harm than the original sin.[1]

At times it's helpful and necessary to confess your secret sins to a trusted friend, minister, or counselor, but in most instances confession is to be made to the person against whom you have sinned and from whom you need forgiveness. There are *secret sins* that we need to confess to God alone because we have wounded only him. And there are *private sins*, by which we have offended one or two people and need to confess our sins discreetly to them. Occasionally there is also a need for *public confession*—when our sins are committed against a group or when a larger number of people have been negatively affected because of our influence. When an entire congregation is wounded by a person's actions or breach of integrity, the sin should be confessed publicly.

When, if ever, should a public figure like a television evangelist or the president of the United States make a public confession? When he or she has committed a sin that becomes public knowledge or should be public knowledge because it affects the ministry or the person's trustworthiness in that role, he or she is right to confess it publicly.

Nobody is perfect. Every leader battles pride, greed, or lust. But when a person in a position of trust commits adultery, embezzles money, develops a drug or alcohol habit, commits an act of violence, or in some other way breaks that trust, he or she should confess that sin publicly and, in most cases, step aside from the public office or role as minister—at least for a period of time. James said, "Not many of you should presume to be teachers, my brothers, because you know that we who teach will be judged more strictly" (James 3:1). If you are in leadership, your actions affect many people, and you must be held to a higher standard. Your prayers and the prayers of your congregation and your nation will be hindered if there is blatant, unconfessed sin. (More about this in chapter 8.)

By the way, if someone has offended you and then comes to you, confessing his sins and humbly asking for forgiveness, you are called to swallow your pride and forgive as Christ forgives you. Remember the parable of the king's servant who was forgiven a great debt? He then turned around and demanded that his fellow servant repay him a small debt. The king was very displeased and severely punished the unjust servant (see Matthew 18:23–35). How can you expect God to show mercy to you and hear your prayers if you are not willing to show mercy to others?

Once you've made every effort to restore a right relationship with others by confessing to them your sins and asking for forgiveness or forgiving their sins toward you, then you can pray with a clear conscience.

RIGHT RELATIONSHIP WITH GOD

James said, "The prayer of a *righteous* man is powerful and effective" (James 5:16; emphasis added). It's true that none of us is completely righteous. We're all sinful creatures made righteous only by the blood of Jesus Christ. But it's also true that the more we live a life of integrity and righteousness, the more powerfully God can flow through us. J. B. Phillips paraphrased the passage this way: "Tremendous power is made available through a good man's earnest prayer."

Prayer is a special privilege for those who are friends of God. Jesus said, "You are my friends if you do what I command" (John 15:14). An omniscient God hears the prayers of every person, regardless of that person's beliefs or behavior; but he only promises power in the prayers of those who are walking with him. When a person, a church, or a nation lives contrary to God's will, the privilege of effective prayer is forfeited.

Solomon observed, "The LORD is far from the wicked but he hears the prayer of the righteous" (Proverbs 15:29). The thief has no right to pray, "Lord, don't let the police catch me." The lazy man who refuses to apply for a job has no right to pray, "Lord, please provide work for me" or, "Please help me with my financial burdens." We have no right to pray, "God, please bless our nation," if we flagrantly disregard his commands.

Norman Vincent Peale told about a time when he was a boy and found a big, black cigar. He slipped behind the barn and lit the cigar. When he heard his father coming, he quickly put it out and tried to act casual. His father began hitching the horses to go into town. When Norman asked his dad if he could accompany him, his father answered firmly: "Son, never make a bold request while harboring a smoldering disobedience."

The psalmist wrote, "If I had cherished sin in my heart, the Lord would not have listened" (Psalm 66:18). Suppose on Friday afternoon your teenager asks for twenty dollars so she can go out with her friends. Are you more likely to give it to her if, in the last few days, she's had a good attitude and a compliant spirit, or if she's spent the last week defying your every request and sneering at your every action? The Bible says, "The LORD detests the sacrifice of the wicked, but the prayer of the upright pleases him" (Proverbs 15:8).

SINCERE PRAYER

James cites Elijah as an example of a person who was heard because of his sincerity:

> Elijah was a man just like us. He prayed earnestly that it would not rain, and it did not rain on the land for three and a half years. Again he prayed, and the heavens gave rain, and the earth produced its crops. (James 5:17)

Elijah warned the nation of Israel that their idolatry and immorality would bring God's judgment. He begged God to bring a severe drought on the nation to awaken them from their spiritual slumber. God granted his request, and a drought set in. Elijah's prayers affected the weather! When the nation repented, Elijah prayed again, and the rains came. (See 1 Kings 17 and 18.)

James says that God heard Elijah's prayer because Elijah prayed earnestly. In the original Greek, James' words were, literally, "He prayed in prayer."

Do you pray in your prayers? A lot of people don't. They just lazily say religious words—their hearts are never really in their prayers.

I have four grandchildren, ages one to eight. They're learning to pray. Their parents teach them to pray at meals, "Dear God, thank you for this food. In Jesus' name, amen." At night, they pray, "Dear God, thank you for Mommy and Daddy, and Nanna and Pop...." Occasionally they get the two prayers mixed up; they sit down to a meal and pray, "Dear God, thank you for Mommy and Daddy...oh, wait!" They catch themselves, giggle, and start over. They had plugged in the wrong tape. We might smile at that in children, but the Lord expects more from mature Christians. God is not impressed with ritual or with prayers that are repeated rotely.

Jesus said, "When you pray, do not keep on babbling like pagans, for they think they will be heard because of their many words" (Matthew 6:7). Pagan worship consisted of repeating chants to their gods over and over again. The people thought there was merit in droning on and on. But Jesus told his followers that prayer was not to be like that. Prayer should be an intimate conversation between two beings who care about each other. Jesus said, "When you pray, go into your room, close the door and pray to your Father, who is unseen. Then your Father, who sees what is done in secret, will reward you" (Matthew 6:6). God is not concerned with verbosity—he's concerned with intensity. It's not the length of your prayer or the cleverness of your words but the sincerity of your heart that matters to God.

When you get a greeting card on a special occasion, what's the most important part of the card? Is it the printed poem or the hand-scribbled note at the bottom? Even if your friend went to great lengths to pick just the right card, the most meaningful part is usually what is personally expressed—from the heart. You can recite memorized prayers to God, and I'm sure God appreciates that somewhat. But the most meaningful prayers are those that express your own thoughts, as awkward and unpoetic as they may be. Those are earnest prayers.

A friend of mine became the new minister of a church that repeated the Lord's Prayer every Sunday. He could tell the practice was more a ritual than a moment of prayer or worship, so one Sunday he substituted a very personal, meaningful pastoral prayer instead. One couple greeted him at the door, irate. "We will not be back!" they said. "They've taken prayer out of the schools, and now you're taking it out of the church!" Jesus intended prayer to be more than a memorized formality, even if it's repeating the Lord's Prayer—or a fingered series of beads we go over and over. Prayer is to be a genuine expression of the soul, a personal conversation with our heavenly Father. Hebrews 11:6 says that God "rewards those who earnestly seek him."

INTENSE PRAYER

James 5:16 in the King James Version reads, "The effectual fervent prayer of a righteous man availeth much." God is more likely to answer your prayer if you ask fervently.

When you're having a casual conversation with your wife or husband, you might allow the television to distract you or a phone call to interrupt you. But if you're asking for something that's important to you, you probably turn off the TV and refuse to answer the phone. It must be difficult for God to think your request is serious when your mind wanders or you refuse to set aside a special time to talk to him about it apart from ringing phones and other demands—or when you're falling asleep.

Jesus was disappointed with his disciples for falling asleep during a prayer time that was important to him. The night he was arrested, the Bible says:

> He said to [his disciples], "My soul is overwhelmed with sorrow to the point of death. Stay here and keep watch with me...."
>
> Then he returned to his disciples and found them sleeping. "Could you men not keep watch with me for one hour?" he asked Peter. "Watch and pray so that you will not fall into temptation. The spirit is willing, but the body is weak." (Matthew 26:38, 40–41)

I'm not saying it's wrong to pray when you're falling asleep. God isn't offended by your sleepy prayer. Suppose you and your mate enjoy talking to one another until one person falls asleep. Those can be intimate times, and you aren't offended if the other person can't stay awake. But if you have something important to discuss, or if you get into an argument, you might sit up in bed and turn the lights on so you can stay awake—so your mate understands that what you have to say is important. In the same way, you might talk to God while you're falling asleep; but important matters should be treated with an appropriate intensity.

Relatives don't fall asleep when the lawyer is reading the will. They're interested in the results. If you're interested in the results of your prayer, you'll stay awake and pay attention.

Let me give you three practical suggestions for praying with greater intensity.

KNEELING

In my daily prayer time, I prefer to kneel. It's harder for my mind to wander, and nearly impossible to fall asleep when I'm on my knees.

PRAYING ALOUD

I also pray aloud whenever possible. I have trouble with silent prayer. My mind goes off on tangents. The worst time for me to pray is often during the Lord's Supper, of all times! When I'm given communion and I'm expected to pray quietly, I have to work hard to prevent my mind from wandering. I begin with good intentions, but usually my prayer goes something like this:

Thank you, Lord, for allowing your body to be broken and your blood to be shed for me. I confess my sins to you. I apologize for thinking lustful thoughts when I watched that television program Friday night. Help me, Lord, to turn off the television and go to bed, starting tonight. Well, tonight we're supposed to go out with friends, and we'll probably get home late if we eat at that same restaurant we did last time. The service there was so slow. I hope we eat someplace different tonight, because I hate waiting so long for a table...

I've gone from the Lord's Supper to my supper in ten seconds! I've learned that I have to choose other times to make serious requests or confessions to God—times when I can pray aloud and not lose my concentration so easily. However, I still do my best to concentrate during communion because I know I need to thank God again for his grace through the body and blood of Christ and for all the other believers who are doing the same.

I think God accepts my simple, lame prayers at communion if there are other times throughout the week when we have more intimate conversations. At my wife's birthday party, I'm going to sing "Happy Birthday" along with everyone else. That's not the time for me to intimately express all my thanks to her the way I should when no one else is around. She's going to be pleased with my singing—even if it's not very good, and maybe even a little perfunctory—as long as there have been private times when I've genuinely expressed how thankful I am for her.

FASTING

The Bible sometimes mentions fasting as an accompaniment to prayer. Jesus didn't command us to fast, but he assumed that at times we would. He gave the following instructions for fasting:

> When you fast, do not look somber as the hypocrites do, for they disfigure their faces to show men they are fasting. I tell you the truth, they have received their reward in full. But when you fast, put oil on your head and wash your face, so that it will not be obvious to men that you are fasting, but only to your Father, who is unseen; and your Father, who sees what is done in secret, will reward you. (Matthew 6:16–18)

Several times the Book of Acts mentions the leaders of the early church fasting before a big decision. For example, Acts 14 says, "Paul and Barnabas appointed elders for them in each church and, with prayer and fasting, committed them to the Lord, in whom they had put their trust" Paul and Barnabas fasted because they intensely wanted God to work through this second generation of leaders, and they wanted to communicate to the elders how important their new role was.

A surefire way to increase the intensity of your prayers is to fast. Kneeling helps your concentration in the short term, but fasting helps for a longer period. It has several benefits:

It's a *demonstration of your seriousness.* You are communicating to God that you're willing to give up food because your request is more important.

It's a *reminder of your priorities.* Fasting reminds you that spiritual things are more important than physical things.

It's also a *reminder to pray.* When your stomach growls, you think, "I'm hungry—oh yes, I'm fasting!" and you take the time to whisper another prayer. When you're fasting, set aside the time you would normally spend eating as time to pray. Fasting then provides a double benefit: Not only are you more intense when you pray, but you also have more time—your normal mealtime—to devote to prayer.

PERSISTENT PRAYER

Jesus told several parables to convey the importance of persistent prayer. One of these is recorded in Luke:

> Suppose one of you has a friend, and he goes to him at midnight and says, "Friend, lend me three loaves of bread, because a friend of mine on a journey has come to me, and I have nothing to set before him."
> Then the one inside answers, "Don't bother me. The door is already locked, and my children are with me in bed. I can't get up and give you anything." I tell you, though he will not get up and give him the bread because he is his friend, yet because of the man's boldness he will get up and give him as much as he needs. (Luke 11:5–8)

Jesus concluded this parable by saying, "So I say to you: Ask and it will be given to you; seek and you will find; knock and the door will be opened to you. For everyone who asks receives; he who seeks finds; and to him who knocks, the door will be opened" (Luke 11:9–10). The words for *ask, seek,* and *knock* are in the present tense, which in the Greek language denotes continual action: Keep on asking, seeking, and knocking. Don't quit praying just because your prayer isn't answered on the first request. Luke recorded another parable that Jesus told so that we would "always pray and not give up" (Luke 18:1). Jesus said:

> In a certain town there was a judge who neither feared God nor cared about men. And there was a widow in that town who kept coming to him with the plea, "Grant me justice against my adversary."
>
> For some time he refused. But finally he said to himself, "Even though I don't fear God or care about men, yet because this widow keeps bothering me, I will see that she gets justice, so that she won't eventually wear me out with her coming!" (Luke 18:2–5)

Even a pagan judge who doesn't care about people will eventually give in to a persistent, poor widow. And a neighbor whose kids and animals are all peacefully sleeping will ruin his night, get up, and answer your request if you keep bugging him. How much more will a loving God respond to the persistent requests of his people?

My wife and I pray together every night before we fall asleep. She is much more gifted at praying than I am. Occasionally one or the other of our sons might call and ask to speak to his mother. If I say, "She's not here, can I give her a message?" he'll respond, "Well, I've got something I wanted her to pray about." I'm tempted to say, "I'm not exactly chopped liver, you know." But I'm not offended because they know Judy is better at praying persistently than I am. I've heard my wife make the same request almost every night for two years. It's for a specific need we have that for some reason God hasn't chosen to answer. She doesn't give up. I just hope God answers before she can be considered a persistent widow!

The point of Jesus' parables is not to compare God with a reluctant, grouchy neighbor or an unrighteous judge; it's to contrast God with them. If an imperfect, stubborn neighbor or an unrighteous judge will eventually give in to a persistent, bold request, how much more will a perfect, loving, generous heavenly Father be anxious to respond to the requests of his children? Jesus wants us to remember that when God says no, it may not be a permanent no.

It may be that God wants us to define and intensify our desires. One of our staff members, David Baird, said that when he would ask his dad for something, his father would often respond, "Half of having is wanting." His dad didn't think he had wanted that toy, that privilege, or that money long enough or badly enough to deserve having it. You can't appreciate a possession or accomplishment adequately if it comes too quickly or too easily. Half of having is wanting.

As Christmas Day or a special birthday nears, your child may begin asking for things he hopes you'll give him. At first he may ask for twenty things. You'll probably wait until your child narrows down the list—refines and intensifies his desires—before you decide what gifts to buy. You don't want to give him his wish only to discover in a few days that it was just a passing whim and wasn't really needed or appreciated.

Tiger Woods won the Masters Golf Tournament at age twenty-one. I doubt he appreciates it as much as Mark

O'Meara, who was forty-one when he won the Masters after fifteen unsuccessful tries. Maybe that's one of the primary reasons God tells us to keep on asking, keep on seeking, keep on knocking. He wants us to fully appreciate what we have. Proverbs 13:12 says, "Hope deferred makes the heart sick, but a longing fulfilled is a tree of life."

Charles H. Spurgeon wrote:

> In the days of flint and steel and brimstone matches we had to strike and strike again, dozens of times, before we could get a spark to live in the tinder; and we were thankful enough if we succeeded at last.
>
> Shall we not be as persevering and hopeful as to heavenly things? We have more certainty of success in this business than we had with our flint and steel, for we have God's promises at our back.
>
> Never let us despair. God's time for mercy will come....Ask in faith, nothing wavering; but never cease from petitioning because the King delays to reply. Strike the steel again. Make the sparks fly and have your tinder ready; you will get a light before long.[2]

I know several people who had prayed about the same thing every day for ten or twenty years—or even longer—before they finally saw their prayer answered. Former University of Louisville basketball coach Denny Crum is a hero in our town because of his accomplishments in the college basketball world. A little over a year ago, he committed his life to Christ, and I had the privilege of baptizing him. A longtime donor of the school told me recently how happy he was that Coach Crum had made a commitment to follow Christ. "I've been praying for twenty-five years that Coach Crum would commit his life to Christ!" he said. I'm so glad he kept praying! One person who wrote to tell me about a prayer God had answered—after twenty-eight years of persistence—concluded her letter, "God does answer prayer, and he knows when the time is right."

BOLD PRAYER

We can learn another lesson from the parable Jesus told of the persistent neighbor. Jesus said the neighbor responded because of the man's *boldness* (see Luke 11:8). It takes a lot of nerve to try to wake up your neighbor in the middle of the night so you can have a midnight snack with a visitor. That's audacious!

When I was a freshman in Bible college, my roommate and I stood looking out the window of our dormitory at a beautiful freshman girl walking by. Not only was she pretty, she was rich—she drove an Impala convertible. That was rare on the Bible college campus. "Wow! I'm going to ask her out!" my roommate said.

Who do you think you are? I thought to myself. *You'd better get ready to get shot down!* Less than two years later they were married! *There's a lesson to be learned here,* I realized. *You have not because you ask not!* So (I had better say this) I determined to be even bolder and set my sights even higher in my prayers for a future mate—and God delivered!

I'm convinced that we don't pray big enough. Jesus said, "I tell you the truth, if anyone says to this mountain, 'Go, throw yourself into the sea,' and does not doubt in his heart but believes that what he says will happen, it will be done for him" (Mark 11:23). A friend of mine showed me a birthday card his sons had given him. It said, "We didn't know what to get you for your birthday, so we asked the Great Weevil. He said, 'A sports car.' Then we asked a small weevil and he said, 'A birthday card.' So we chose the lesser of two weevils!" We don't usually ask for big things. We choose the little requests, which seem easier to fulfill—and less disappointing if they go unanswered. They demand less faith from us too.

One of the reasons Southeast has been blessed so abundantly by God is that our elders have been bold. They have a slogan: "We are going to try something so big that if God isn't in it, it will fail." We've tried a lot of big things, and some of them have failed. But more often than not, God has blessed those audacious requests, and we've seen some mighty big answers to prayer. Long ago I memorized a verse by John Newton about asking largely of God:

> Thou art coming to a King,
> Large petitions with thee bring;
> For His grace and power are such
> None can ever ask too much!

CORPORATE PRAYER

Someone asked me, "If hundreds of people pray for you, is God more likely to answer than if just one person prays?" I think so. Jesus said, "If two of you on earth agree about anything you ask for, it will be done for you by my Father in heaven. For where two or three come together in my name, there am I with them" (Matthew 18:19–20).

Frank Peretti in his novels often portrays angels poised to fight spiritual battles on behalf of believers, but they're unable to come without sufficient prayer support from other believers. Peretti's imagery is rooted in a passage found in Daniel 10. For twenty-one days Daniel prayed and fasted, wanting to understand a vision God had shown him. After the twenty-one days, a mighty figure of a man appeared before him. The man was a powerful angel; some speculate that he may have been the Son of God himself. The man said to Daniel:

> Do not be afraid, Daniel. Since the first day that you set your mind to gain understanding and to humble yourself before your God, your words were heard, and I have come in response to them. But the prince of the Persian kingdom resisted me twenty-one days. Then Michael, one of the chief princes, came to help me, because I was detained there with the king of Persia. (Daniel 10:12–13)

The mighty angelic being had set out to help Daniel the very day he began praying. But a demonic force—the prince of the Persian kingdom—had attempted to stop him. This angelic warfare was being conducted in another dimension, away from human eyes. But it was occurring nonetheless, and the Scripture indicates that the comings and goings of angels and demons were affected by the prayers of the saints.

If one person asks me to visit a relative who is in the hospital, I might honor the request. But if fifty people call and say it would mean a lot to the hospitalized person for me to visit, I'll go right away! Scripture doesn't say for sure, but I believe God is more likely to intervene in the affairs of men when his saints petition him together to do so.

Shortly after Dallas Theological Seminary was founded in 1924, the school came to the point of bankruptcy. Its creditors had banded together and threatened to foreclose at noon on a particular day. That morning, the founders of the school met in the president's office to pray that God would provide. In the meeting was a well-known preacher from Chicago named Harry Ironside. When his turn came to pray, he did so in a characteristically refreshing manner: "Lord, we know that the cattle on a thousand hills are Thine. Please sell some of them and send us the money."

While they were praying, a Texas cattleman came into the business office and said, "I just sold two carloads of cattle in Fort Worth. I've been trying to make a business deal go through, and it won't work, and I feel that God is compelling me to give this money to the seminary. I don't know if you need it or not, but here's the check."

A secretary, knowing something of the financial seriousness of the hour, went to the door of the prayer meeting and timidly tapped. Dr. Lewis Chafer responded, took the check out of her hand, and saw that it was for the exact amount of the school's debt. When he looked at the signature and noted that it was a cattle rancher, he looked at Dr. Ironside and said, "Harry, God sold the cattle!"[3]

Dallas Theological Seminary has remained open for the past seventy-five years and has trained hundreds of effective ministers and Christian leaders for the kingdom of God. God still answers prayer!

Part Two

GOD
ANSWERS
PRAYER
DRAMATICALLY

Chapter Four

GOD ANSWERED PRAYER
DRAMATICALLY IN BIBLE TIMES

*The smoke of the incense, together with the prayers of the
saints, went up before God from the angel's hand.*

—Revelation 8:4

Jeff and Teresa Bowling recently moved to Louisville from
Lexington, where they had been members of Southland
Christian Church. They visited several churches in Louisville
and really liked our church, but they couldn't decide if that
was where God wanted them to be. They wondered if perhaps
God wanted them to find a congregation where they could
become involved in leadership more quickly.

One day while traveling on a business trip to Minnesota,
Jeff prayed, "Lord, give me a sign that it's your will for us to
join Southeast Christian Church." Minutes later, in the
Minneapolis airport, he looked up and saw me walking up to
the gate! He couldn't believe it. "Lord," he said, "that's good
enough for me!" Jeff introduced himself to me and
explained his prayer. "Bob, do you think God is giving me a
confirmation about your church?" he asked.

I laughed and said, "Without question!" The following
week they became members.

Under normal circumstances, the odds would certainly be stacked against Jeff's running into me at the Minneapolis airport. But what makes the story even more amazing is that I wasn't scheduled to be on that flight. I had been forced to make an emergency trip home from a speaking engagement in Spokane, Washington, to preach for the funeral of a long-time friend.

We serve a God who has the power to answer our prayers—even in dramatic ways at times. Nothing is impossible for God. There are some qualifiers, as I've mentioned. God doesn't guarantee that he'll answer all of our prayers exactly the way we ask, or prayer would put us in charge of the universe. That would be dangerous! Sometimes God uses natural means to answer our prayers, as we discussed in Part 1 of this book. God moves mountains more often through gradual erosion than through volcanic eruption. And sometimes God expects us to use our own resources—dynamite and bulldozers in addition to our prayers—to move the mountain. But God does promise that if we pray, trusting in him, there will be times when he will do spectacular, even miraculous, seemingly impossible things to answer our requests.

In this chapter, let's consider some examples from Scripture where God answered prayer in dramatic ways.

FINDING ISAAC'S FUTURE WIFE

Isaac was of marrying age, and his father, Abraham, was concerned. Abraham took his servant aside and said, "I want my son to marry a young woman from among my people. She needs to be familiar with our customs and our beliefs. I don't want him marrying any of these Canaanite girls. Go back to our homeland and find a suitable wife for him."

Have you ever arranged a blind date? That's a lot of pressure! You probably waited anxiously by the phone to hear how it went. Imagine arranging a blind marriage. Abraham's servant had a huge responsibility. The family loaded him down with gifts to make it more likely the girl would say yes (it took ten camels to carry all the gifts!), and Abraham sent him off.

When the servant arrived at the watering hole outside Abraham's hometown, he stopped and asked God for help. He prayed:

> O LORD, God of my master Abraham, give me success today, and show kindness to my master Abraham. See, I am standing beside this spring, and the daughters of the townspeople are coming out to draw water. May it be that when I say to a girl, "Please let down your jar that I may have a drink," and she says, "Drink, and I'll water your camels too"—let her be the one you have chosen for your servant Isaac. By this I will know that you have shown kindness to my master. (Genesis 24:12–14)

The servant prayed a specific prayer and asked for an obvious sign. "May the right girl not only offer me a drink, but offer to water my camels too."

Do you know how much water a thirsty camel can drink at one time? Thirty gallons! Camels are walking reservoirs. God designed them to be the cargo ships of the desert.

Let's be conservative and say the camels were only half empty. That would mean each camel would need fifteen gallons of water to be satisfied. Fifteen gallons times ten camels—that's 150 gallons of water! Conservatively estimating! If a bucket held five gallons of water (and that would be a hefty bucket for a young girl to carry), she would have to draw thirty buckets of water from the well. That's no small task! The servant knew it was highly unlikely that a young girl would make such an offer, so if she did, it would be a dramatic sign from God that she was the right one. It would have to be a special girl who would volunteer to draw enough water for a stranger's camels.

Occasionally it's appropriate to ask God for a sign to affirm or deny an answer to prayer. Sometimes demanding such a sign can be an act of cowardice or lack of faith on our part, so we need to be cautious about doing such things. But there are times when we're trying to discern between several good choices (when all the options are obviously within God's will, according to his Word), and we'd really like to have some confirmation from God about the right decision. At such times it's not wrong to humbly ask God for some direction, as Jeff Bowling did in the story I told at the beginning of this chapter, and as Abraham's servant did. The Bible tells us what happened next:

> As he was still speaking to the Lord about this, a beautiful young girl named Rebekah arrived with a water jug on her shoulder and filled it at the spring....Running over to her, the servant asked her for a drink.

"Certainly, sir," she said, and quickly lowered the jug for him to drink. Then she said, "I'll draw water for your camels, too, until they have enough!" So she emptied the jug into the watering trough and ran down to the spring again and kept carrying water to the camels until they had enough. The servant said no more, but watched her carefully to see if she would finish the job, so that he would know whether she was the one. Then at last, when the camels had finished drinking, he produced a quarter-ounce gold earring and two five-ounce golden bracelets for her wrists. (Genesis 24:15–22 TLB)

The servant asked, "Who are you?" When he discovered that Rebekah was from Abraham's tribe, he was elated. Now all he had to do was convince Rebekah and her family that she was the one for Isaac. But before he headed to Rebekah's house, he took the time to thank God for dramatically answering his prayer.

The man stood there a moment with head bowed, worshiping Jehovah. "Thank you, Lord God of my master Abraham," he prayed; "thank you for being so kind and true to him, and for leading me straight to the family of my master's relatives." (Genesis 24:26–27 TLB)

Rebekah and her family could see that God was at work, and she agreed to go to meet Isaac. Within a week, Isaac and Rebekah were married, and the Bible says Isaac loved her (Genesis 24:67).

This would be an example of a dramatic answer to prayer but not necessarily a miracle, because it was not a visible, supernatural event. But when you consider that a beautiful, unmarried, congenial, hardworking virgin was willing to relocate to marry a man she had never met, that's quite near miraculous!

CALLING DOWN FIRE FROM HEAVEN

Elijah the prophet got into a heated debate with Ahab, king of Israel. It hadn't rained in Israel for three years, so everyone was a little on edge. The king's wife, Jezebel, was at the center of the controversy because she had imported her worship of Baal when she came into the marriage. The people had become immoral, and the country no longer had any spiritual compass. God's judgment came as a result of Eljiah's earnest prayer that it wouldn't rain until the people repented. So in typical political spin, Ahab blamed the famine on the praying prophet. When Elijah came to appear before him, Ahab said, "Is that you, you troubler of Israel?" (1 Kings 18:17). Sometimes the Bible leaves out details. I think the scene probably unfolded like this:

"The very idea that worship of Baal has been responsible for this famine is just absurd," Ahab ranted. "Elijah, prophets like you are a plague on this progressive society. You are narrow-minded and bigoted. One god is just as good as another."

"OK, king, let's have a contest," the feisty prophet Elijah replied. "You gather your 850 priests of Baal and meet me on Mount Carmel for a battle of the gods."

"Fine, you're on," Ahab snapped.

Word about the contest spread, and a huge crowd gathered on Mount Carmel to watch the spectacle.

Elijah announced the rules of the contest. Each side was to build an altar to their respective gods. "You build an altar to Baal," Elijah said, "and I'll build one to the God of Israel, the God our forefathers worshiped, the one true God who led us out of Egypt. We'll pile some wood on the altar and place an animal sacrifice on top.

"But here's the catch," Elijah continued. "Nobody lights a fire. You pray to Baal to burn up your sacrifice. I'll pray to Jehovah God to burn up my sacrifice. The god who responds with fire from heaven will be declared the champion—the only true God. Fair enough?"

They agreed.

"You first," Elijah said.

The prophets of Baal built their altar and prayed all morning. No fire came from heaven.

About noontime, Elijah began mocking them.

"You'll have to shout louder than that," he scoffed, "to catch the attention of your god! Perhaps he is talking to someone, or is out sitting on the toilet, or maybe he is away on a trip, or is asleep and needs to be wakened!"

So they shouted louder and, as was their custom, cut themselves with knives and swords until the blood gushed out. They raved all afternoon until the time of the evening sacrifice, but there was no reply, no voice, no answer. (1 Kings 18:27–29 TLB)

Finally, toward evening, Elijah interrupted. "Time's up," he said. "That's enough. It's my turn."

Elijah built an altar, placed some wood on top, and laid the meat of the bull he had slaughtered on top of the wood.

Then, to add to the drama, he dug a trench around the altar. The crowd began to murmur. "What's he doing?" "I don't know." "He's up to something."

To the astonishment of the crowd, he then commanded some volunteers from the audience to pour water on the altar. Water was scarce—there had been a three-year drought. But they did what he asked. When they were finished dousing the altar, Elijah said, "That's not wet enough. Do it again!" They doused it again. "One more time!" Elijah barked.

By the time they were finished pouring water on the altar, the wood was soaked and water filled the trough Elijah had dug around the altar.

Elijah then prayed a simple, earnest prayer to God:

O LORD, God of Abraham, Isaac and Israel, let it be known today that you are God in Israel and that I am your servant and have done all these things at your command. Answer me, O LORD, answer me, so these people will know that you, O LORD, are God, and that you are turning their hearts back again. (1 Kings 18:36–37)

It was a short and simple prayer. You can read it in less than fifteen seconds. But that's all it took for God to hear Elijah's request.

Then the fire of the LORD fell and burned up the sacrifice, the wood, the stones and the soil, and also licked up the water in the trench.

When all the people saw this, they fell prostrate and cried, "The LORD—he is God! The LORD—he is God!" (1 Kings 18:38–39)

What a miraculous, instantaneous answer to a simple prayer of faith! The Bible says that Elijah was not a superman—he was a man just like us (see James 5:17), but he believed God could do miraculous things through prayer. Prayer doesn't have to be flowery, long, or filled with theological jargon—it just needs to be intense, sincere, and real.

ESCAPE FROM AN IMPOSSIBLE SITUATION

Unlike most politicians of his day, King Hezekiah was a righteous ruler. The Bible says, "He did what was right in the eyes of the LORD" (2 Kings 18:3). In fact, he was the greatest king since the divided kingdom.

> Hezekiah trusted in the LORD, the God of Israel. There was no one like him among all the kings of Judah, either before him or after him. He held fast to the LORD and did not cease to follow him....And the LORD was with him; he was successful in whatever he undertook. (2 Kings 18:5–7)

Then one day, in the fourteenth year of Hezekiah's administration, the powerful Assyrian army descended on Jerusalem like a threatening black cloud. Hundreds of thousands of barbarian soldiers, who had already ravaged every city in their path, camped around Jerusalem and made ready to rape and pillage the capital. The arrogant Assyrian king, Sennacherib, sent a sarcastic letter to Hezekiah:

> Don't be fooled by that god you trust in. Don't believe it when he says that I won't conquer Jerusalem. You know

perfectly well what the kings of Assyria have done wherever they have gone; they have completely destroyed everything. Why would you be any different? Have the gods of the other nations delivered them? (2 Kings 19:10–12 TLB)

When Hezekiah read the letter, he was distraught. He took the letter to the temple and spread it out before the Lord, as if to say, "Here it is, Lord. What do you want me to do about it?" Then he prayed this prayer:

O LORD, God of Israel, enthroned between the cherubim, you alone are God over all the kingdoms of the earth. You have made heaven and earth. Give ear, O LORD, and hear; open your eyes, O LORD, and see; listen to the words Sennacherib has sent to insult the living God.

It is true, O LORD, that the Assyrian kings have laid waste these nations and their lands. They have thrown their gods into the fire and destroyed them, for they were not gods but only wood and stone, fashioned by men's hands. Now, O LORD our God, deliver us from his hand, so that all kingdoms on earth may know that you alone, O LORD, are God. (2 Kings 19:14–19)

If ever you get trapped in an impossible situation and there's no way out, do what Hezekiah did. Take it to the Lord in prayer. Say, as Hezekiah did, "Lord, this is too big for me. I can't handle this on my own. You'll have to take charge, or I'm done."

God answered Hezekiah's prayer in a most dramatic way. What seemed like an impossible situation was eliminated by morning. That night, the angel of the Lord visited the Assyrian camp and put to death 185,000 men in the Assyrian camp! When the rest of the Assyrian soldiers awakened the next morning, they were surrounded by dead bodies. The Bible says simply, "So Sennacherib king of Assyria broke camp and withdrew. He returned to Nineveh and stayed there" (2 Kings 19:36). I guess so! Losing 185,000 men would hurt most armies. Sennacherib went scurrying home like a wounded animal with his tail between his legs, wondering what had just happened. Hezekiah and the city of Jerusalem were spared. They had won the victory without throwing a spear or losing a single Israeli soldier.

HEALING FROM A DEADLY ILLNESS

The next chapter, 2 Kings 20, reports another dramatic answer to one of Hezekiah's prayers:

> In those days Hezekiah became ill and was at the point of death. The prophet Isaiah son of Amoz went to him and said, "This is what the LORD says: 'Put your house in order, because you are going to die; you will not recover.'" (2 Kings 20:1)

God is not a cruel practical joker. He is always truthful. God informed King Hezekiah that his sickness was terminal and that it was time for him to make final arrangements— write out the will, call the funeral home, say good-bye to loved ones. Hezekiah knew God doesn't say what he doesn't mean. His time to die had come. Yet Hezekiah believed he could change God's mind:[1] "Hezekiah turned his face to the wall and prayed to the LORD" (2 Kings 20:2).

Maybe he turned his face to the wall because he didn't want the nurses to see the tears streaming down his face. No matter how powerful you are, it's a frightening experience to be told you're going to die. Woody Allen once said he didn't fear death—he just didn't want to be there when it happened. The king didn't want to die. He was still a relatively young man. So he pleaded with God to reconsider. "'Remember, O LORD, how I have walked before you faithfully and with wholehearted devotion and have done what is good in your eyes.' And Hezekiah wept bitterly" (2 Kings 20:3).

God heard Hezekiah's prayer and answered it dramatically.

Before Isaiah had left the middle court, the word of the LORD came to him: "Go back and tell Hezekiah, the leader of my people, 'This is what the LORD, the God of your father David, says: I have heard your prayer and seen your tears; I will heal you. On the third day from now you will go up to the temple of the LORD. I will add fifteen years to your life.'" (2 Kings 20:4–6)

Sometimes, for reasons we'll discuss later, our prayers need to be prolonged vigils accompanied by days of fasting. But God answers brief, intense, tearful prayers too. Before the prophet even left the king's property, God sent him back with a different message. Again, just as he did with Moses, God changed his mind as to how he would deal with one of his children because the child prayed. Prayer can make a difference in what happens.

When Isaiah went back to the king's chambers and told him the good news, Hezekiah asked, "How can I be sure this is a word from the Lord and it's true?"

"Would you like for the sun's shadow on the floor to go forward ten steps or backward ten steps?" Isaiah offered.

"It would be a more dramatic miracle for the shadow to reverse itself ten steps," the king replied.

"OK," Isaiah said, "that will be your sign that God has heard your prayer." And the shadow did move backward ten steps! (See 2 Kings 20:8–11.)

You might expect the Bible to say, "Hezekiah lived happily ever after." But the story doesn't have a happy ending. Hezekiah's last fifteen years were counterproductive. You'd think he would spend those years in grateful service to God and make every minute count. But Hezekiah made at least two serious mistakes that negatively impacted the entire nation.

The first incident happened almost immediately after Hezekiah was healed, when some visitors arrived from Babylon. They had heard that Hezekiah was ill and had come bearing sympathy and a gift from the king of Babylon. Hezekiah proudly showed them around Jerusalem, boasting about the treasuries of the palace and the weapons in his armory. He thought he was impressing them, but he only provoked his enemies to envy him—and he gave away some important military secrets in the process. When the visitors left, Isaiah came back to the palace with another word from the Lord. He told Hezekiah that because of his prideful display,

> The time will surely come when everything in your palace, and all that your fathers have stored up until this day, will be carried off to Babylon. Nothing will be left, says the LORD. And some of your descendants, your own flesh and blood, that will be born to you, will be taken away, and they will become eunuchs in the palace of the king of Babylon. (2 Kings 20:17–18)

God's judgment did come upon Hezekiah's descendants, as the Bible records a few chapters later:

> In the eighth year of the reign of the king of Babylon, he took Jehoiachin [king of Judah] prisoner. As the LORD had declared, Nebuchadnezzar removed all the treasures from the temple of the LORD and from the royal palace, and took away all the gold articles that Solomon king of Israel had made for the temple of the LORD. He carried into exile all Jerusalem: all the officers and fighting men, and all the craftsmen and artisans—a total of ten thousand. Only the poorest people of the land were left. (2 Kings 24:12–14)

Hezekiah's second mistake may or may not have been completely under his control. During that fifteen-year extension of his life, Hezekiah fathered a child named Manasseh, who became the most wicked king that ever ruled Judah. Hezekiah might have been a perfect parent to Manasseh. Sometimes even great parents have rebellious kids, because every person has his or her own free will to make good or bad choices. But more than likely, Hezekiah, in his old age, neglected his young son or overindulged him (or both), and didn't discipline him properly. Manasseh did despicable things as king and brought the nation to an all-time moral low.

If God chooses to answer your prayer in a dramatic way, don't use that experience as an excuse for spiritual pride and complacency. Just because you're in the will of God one day doesn't mean you have a license for immorality and indifference in the next. The Bible warns, "If you think you are standing firm, be careful that you don't fall!" (1 Corinthians 10:12).

FREEDOM FOR AN IMPRISONED APOSTLE

King Herod arrested some members of the early church and even had one of their pastors—James—executed. Herod saw that his actions made him popular among the local Jewish leaders, the majority of whom were hostile to Christianity. So he had another key Christian leader— Simon Peter—arrested as well. He intended to bring Peter to trial and, presumably, to put him to death.

The Bible says, "Peter was kept in prison, but the church was earnestly praying to God for him" (Acts 12:5). The congregation of saints had a spontaneous, intense prayer meeting for Simon Peter. Surely they prayed that he would be courageous and maintain his faith and that his life would be spared.

God answered the believers' prayers miraculously. That night while Peter was sleeping, guarded by four soldiers, an angel appeared quietly in his cell. The angel slapped him on the side to awaken him and whispered, "Quick! Get up!" Instantly, the chains fell off Peter's wrists.

"Get dressed and follow me," the angel urged, and Peter left with the heavenly visitor, thinking at first that he was only dreaming. They passed the first and second cellblocks and came to the iron gate that opened onto the city street. The gate opened by itself! They didn't have laser beams or automatic gates in that day—this was a miracle. The angel accompanied Peter down the street for about a block, then left him. Suddenly Peter realized what had happened. *I'm not dreaming—it's really true!* he thought to himself. *The Lord has sent his angel to save me!*

Peter headed to the home of Mary, the mother of John Mark, where he knew people were gathered for a prayer meeting—praying for him. Imagine what he must have been thinking along the way. *I can't wait to tell them what just happened. They're not going to believe the way God answered their prayers! I can't wait to see their faces.* Peter arrived at Mary's house and knocked on the front door.

A servant girl named Rhoda came to answer the door. When she recognized Peter's voice, she was so overjoyed she ran back without opening it and exclaimed, "Peter is at the door!"

"You're out of your mind," they told her. When she kept insisting that it was so, they said, "It must be his angel."

But Peter kept on knocking, and when they opened the door and saw him, they were astonished. (Acts 12:13–16)

Isn't that typical? We pray, and then we're utterly astonished when God answers. We pray for a sick person to get well, then leave the room and mumble sadly, "I don't think he's going to make it." When our teenagers start driving, we pray that God will keep them safe. Then we pace the floor when they're two minutes late and mutter, "I just know they've had an accident." We pray for the Lord to forgive our sins and then murmur, "I'm not sure God has forgiven me—I'm afraid to die."

Dr. Fred Craddock tells about a preacher who visited a critically ill woman in the hospital. She was so weak that she was unable to get out of bed. The minister talked with the woman for a while and then offered a prayer to God that she would be healed.

The sick woman thanked him and said, "You know, I'm beginning to feel better already. I haven't felt this good in months!"

She sat up and started to get out of bed, but the preacher objected. "Maybe you'd better lie back down."

The woman insisted on getting up, and she proceeded to put on her slippers and walk around the room, saying, "Preacher, your prayer worked! Hallelujah! I've been healed!" She started laughing and praising God. She threw her arms around the stunned preacher and gave him a big hug.

When the minister left, he walked to his car, sat in the

driver's seat, put his head on the steering wheel, and said, "Lord, don't you ever do that to me again!"

SHAKING THINGS UP IN PRISON

Paul and Silas were arrested for preaching about Jesus in the city of Philippi. They were beaten, severely flogged, and then shackled in a damp, dark, inner dungeon inside the prison. Historian John McRay describes what Paul and Silas probably experienced:

> Roman imprisonment was preceded by being stripped naked and then flogged, a humiliating, painful, and bloody ordeal. The bleeding wounds went untreated; prisoners sat in painful leg or wrist chains. Mutilated, bloodstained clothing was not replaced, even in the cold of winter....
>
> Most cells were dark, especially the inner cells of a prison, like the one Paul and Silas inhabited in Philippi. Unbearable cold, lack of water, cramped quarters, and sickening stench from few toilets made sleeping difficult and waking hours miserable....Because of the miserable conditions, many prisoners begged for a speedy death. Others simply committed suicide.[2]

If there were an Internet site with a dungeon-cam on Paul and Silas, what would you expect to hear? Complaints, cursing, and painful moans. Instead—they sang! And prayed. The Bible says, "About midnight Paul and Silas were praying and singing hymns to God, and the other prisoners were listening to them" (Acts 16:25).

If you're familiar with the story, you know what happened next: "Suddenly there was such a violent earthquake that the foundations of the prison were shaken. At once all the prison doors flew open, and everybody's chains came loose" (Acts 16:26). Paul and Silas's prayer produced an earthquake that shook open the prison doors and unlocked their shackles. Not only were the prisoners freed, but the jailer gave his life to Christ. He and his family were baptized right there, in the middle of the night. This particular answer to prayer was so dramatic that it impressed an unbeliever and converted him to Christ.

These examples from Scripture prove two things: God has the power to answer prayer; and sometimes he does it in very dramatic—even supernatural—ways. The Bible says that nothing is impossible for God (see Mark 10:27), and that when we pray, nothing is impossible for us (see Matthew 17:20). E. M. Bounds said, "Prayer can do anything God can do." But is that still true today? Does God still answer prayer dramatically today? Let's see.

Chapter Five

GOD ANSWERS PRAYER DRAMATICALLY TODAY

Prayer can do anything God can do.
—E. M. Bounds

I heard about a mother and her children who were taking a tour of New York City and were in awe of St. Patrick's Cathedral. The children were especially curious about the votive candles at the front of the cathedral, so the mother invited each of them to light one. She explained that it was customary to say a prayer of petition or thanks as the candles were being lit. "These are not like birthday candles," she said. "You're not making a wish but asking for God's blessings."

After the family bowed for a prayer, they began to walk away. The mother asked the kids if they had any questions about what they had just experienced. "No," said the five-year-old, "but if there's a pony outside, it's mine!"

God is not like Santa Claus—waiting to make our wishes come true. But as we've discussed, God is a loving father who wants to give good gifts to his children. Jesus said, "If you have faith as small as a mustard seed, you can say to this mountain, 'Move from here to there' and it will move.

Nothing will be impossible for you" (Matthew 17:20). That's a spectacular promise! Nothing is impossible for God. And God is the same God yesterday, today, and forever. What he did in the Old Testament and in the New Testament, he still does today. God still answers prayer dramatically and miraculously. Here are some modern-day examples.

POWERFUL PRAYERS OF THE ELDERS

Eleven-year-old Mary Whitlock had been experiencing seizures since she was an infant. Medicine and even brain surgery had not resolved the problem. In the summer of 2002, she was suffering twenty to twenty-five seizures per day. Because of her condition she was not allowed to swim, attend parties, or do many other fun things with her friends that eleven-year-olds long to do.

Just before school began in August, her Sunday school teacher—Jim Hunt, who is also an elder in our church—suggested that the elders anoint her with oil and pray for her according to James 5:14. After the elders prayed, Mary's little sister added her own petition: "Please, God, don't let Mary have any more seizures." With the exception of one day when Mary was battling strep throat, she has not had a seizure since those prayers.

This idea of the elders anointing the sick person with oil and praying for healing deserves special attention. James wrote, "Is any one of you sick? He should call the elders of the church to pray over him and anoint him with oil in the name of the Lord" (James 5:14). The Greek word *astheneō*, here translated "sick," suggests extreme illness. It refers to those who are without strength or are to the point of being incapacitated. We certainly ought to pray even when we are mildly ill, but James is referring in that passage to seriously ill people. That's why he recommends the elders going to the sick person's side rather than the individual coming to the leaders. He talks about the elders "praying over him," implying that the person is bedridden. James doesn't intend that elders only pray over those who are bedridden, but he gives us this imagery because most seriously ill people will be confined to their beds.

A distinct, extraordinary power flows from God when elders join in prayer over a sick person. In the next verse James promises, "And the prayer offered in faith will make the sick person well; the Lord will raise him up" (James 5:15). The prayer of the elders is not a magic formula that guarantees healing. Those who suggest otherwise deny both Scripture and experience. God frequently used Paul to heal the sick, yet the great apostle said, "I left Trophimus sick in Miletus" (2 Timothy 4:20), and he spoke of his own "thorn in the flesh" (2 Corinthians 12:7). Not everyone Paul prayed for was healed. We've anointed some people with oil and prayed for them, and they still died. But many others have experienced dramatic healing.

We're not sure exactly what James meant when he

commanded the elders to "anoint the sick person with oil." Was this anointing medicinal or ceremonial? It may have been simply symbolic of the Holy Spirit's presence. When a very ill person in our congregation asks the elders to pray over him or her, a few of them will gather around. One elder takes a small amount of olive oil and touches the sick person's forehead with it, and then they pray. We're using the oil to symbolize the Holy Spirit's presence and to demonstrate our desire to be obedient to God. But the general feeling from Bible scholars about this passage is that the oil to which James referred was medicinal. Charles Swindoll wrote:

> The specific Greek term used in James 5:14 for anointing does not convey the thought of a religious ceremony in which oil is applied to the head. Here it means to "apply or to rub something into the skin." In biblical times, oil was used on one who was sick for its medicinal effects. We find this occurring in Luke 10:34 when the Samaritan poured oil and wine onto the wounds of the man victimized by robbers and left for dead.
>
> James does not write about ceremonial anointing; what he called for was the use of the best medicinal procedure of the day, simply rubbing or massaging oil into the body and then praying. Translating into today's terms, oil represents antibiotics, various other medications, surgery, therapy and so on.[1]

Instead of encouraging "faith healing" apart from the use of medicine, James taught the opposite: When you're sick, get the best medical treatment and apply it, then call for the spiritual leaders of the church and have them pray.

My grandson Charlie had a strange illness several years ago. Following a fall in a patio area, where he knocked out his two front teeth, he developed an infection that eventually caused a lymph node to swell badly. The doctors were concerned about the lump under his jaw and scheduled surgery to remove and test the lymph node. But before the surgery could be performed, Charlie developed cellulitis and had to undergo emergency surgery, followed by a week of hospitalization. We were all very nervous about Charlie's health, and the doctors struggled to discover the problem. Although aggressive antibiotic treatments shrank the swelling, it still wasn't completely gone.

A second, more risky surgery was planned to remove the lymph node. We called for the elders. They came, anointed Charlie with oil, and prayed for him. Within a few weeks the lymph node inexplicably returned to its normal size, and surgery was not needed. Charlie has been a healthy young boy now for six years, and we praise God for answered prayer.

Fifteen years ago, the elders prayed for our stewardship minister, Mike Graham, who just before joining our staff was told he had cancer and only had six months to live. He has been faithfully serving the Lord on our staff for fifteen years! There is special power when elders gather to pray for a sick person.

But it's not just when elders pray that God answers in dramatic ways. There are scores of examples of everyday

Christian people who prayed to God for specific needs and saw God answer in dramatic ways. Here are just a few.

MISSION SCHOOL FIRE ESCAPE

The Rodeo-Chediski forest fire devastated much of Arizona in 2002, consuming nearly half a million acres. Firefighters labored valiantly to save the American Indian Christian Mission, but they were forced to leave when the blaze became too dangerous. Prayers from people in the area and all over the state were lifted up to God, asking him to spare the mission. The fire came within a few feet of the mission school on three sides, yet not one building was touched. Three crosses stood near the entrance to the school. Only the one in the middle was burned. To those in the mission, that lone burned cross was a reminder—a sign—that Jesus Christ had saved the mission, as he has saved our souls.[2]

DRAMATIC RESCUE AT SEA

Years ago I met a man named Earl Feathers, an elder at First Christian Church in Kingsport, Tennessee. He confirmed a dramatic story about his daughter, Sandy, that had been printed in *Guideposts* magazine.

Sandy and her husband, Joe, were sailing in the Gulf of Mexico when they were caught in an unexpected storm. The gales blew them far out into the open sea. When the storm subsided, they drifted helplessly for two days, baking in the hot sun. Their water supply dwindled away, and they knew their lives were in danger.

The couple prayed to God for help, but no help came. On the third day, Joe was so weakened and disheartened that he gave up and lay down in the shell of the tiny craft, accepting that they would soon die.

In that moment of despair Sandy looked down at their little dog that had been on the sailboat with them throughout the ordeal. The dog looked up at her with total trust. Sandy prayed one more time, "Oh Lord, as my dog trusts me as his master, so I put my total trust in you. You are our only hope. Please deliver us."

Just then she looked up and saw in the distance what appeared to be a cross coming toward them. She thought she must be hallucinating and blinked to clear her vision; but there was indeed a cross on the horizon. She awakened Joe. He, too, could make out a cross moving in their direction.

As the cross neared, they could see that it was actually the masthead of a large yacht—and it was coming their way! The couple stood up, waving their arms to attract attention. The boat kept heading directly for them, and they soon feared it might slice their small sailboat in two and kill them in an ironic accident.

But as the ship came dangerously near, they saw a young boy peering over the rail. When he saw their frantic waves, he disappeared briefly and returned with his father, pointing toward the stranded couple.

The yacht pulled alongside and hauled them aboard. When they were safely on deck, Sandy said, "It's incredible that you found us! We thought we'd never be rescued!" But what the yacht owner explained next convinced Joe and Sandy that their rescue was no accident. The yacht had been traveling on automatic pilot for several hours, but inexplicably the man and his son were ten miles off their intended course! God had heard the couple's prayer and answered dramatically by guiding the yacht directly to them.[3]

HEALING OF A MAN WITH LEUKEMIA

I've seen several dramatic examples of healing as a result of prayer with members of our congregation. I mentioned earlier how God answered our prayers for Brett DeYoung. Another dramatic answer to prayer occurred in the life of Mark Fryman, who was not yet thirty years old when he was diagnosed with leukemia and told he might not live another six months. Mark went through two bone marrow transplants and was quarantined in a hospital in Seattle. His body became terribly emaciated and nearly gave in to the disease. Three times the doctors warned him and his wife, Mary, that he might not live through the night. Each time, Mary called family, friends, and the members of their adult Bible Fellowship class at Southeast, and they held all-night prayer vigils. Each time, Mark survived. To the doctors' surprise, Mark began to regain his strength. He returned home a few weeks later. Today Mark is fully recovered, back at work, and active again in the church.

OPENING OF A BARREN WOMB

My son Rusty and his wife, Kellie, were saddened at being unable to have a second child. The doctors had told Kellie that Charlie, our first grandchild, was a miracle and that she might never have another baby. They prayed and went to a fertility specialist, but nothing helped. They began pursuing adoption, but each effort fell through. For several years they tried to add to their family but met with disappointment each time.

When a friend of mine—a popular evangelist—came to speak at Southeast, I remembered that he had told me fifteen years earlier that he believed God had gifted him to pray for infertile couples. "I know you're going to think this is strange," he had confided in private. "But I've prayed for dozens of couples who were infertile, and God has given them children. God doesn't always answer my prayers, but more often than not, he does." He had scores of pictures and letters to verify God's answers. This man is not a "faith healer" and doesn't even promote publicly the gift he believes God has given him. In fact, his expertise and passion are in an entirely different arena.

I asked my friend if he would pray for Rusty and Kellie. He huddled with them in a side room before the service began and prayed that God would give them another child. Two months later, Kellie became pregnant with our grandson Tommy. Less than a year after Tommy's birth, Kellie became pregnant again, this time with Kimberly. I've wondered whether I should call my friend back and tell him to amend that prayer before things get out of hand!

SNAGGING THE SNIPERS

John Allen Muhammad and Lee Malvo were the suspected snipers who had killed ten people and wounded three others in the area around our nation's capital in the fall of 2002. You may have read or seen on the news the dramatic story of how truck driver Ron Lantz called 911 after spotting the suspects' car at a rest stop. While the unsuspecting men slept in their vehicle, Mr. Lantz and his friends blocked the exits and waited for the police to arrive.

You may not have heard from the national news media about the prayer meeting that preceded that capture. One week earlier, Mr. Lantz and fellow truckers had been discussing the sniper case over their CBs. "Finally, Lantz and several others told everybody to pull off the road," columnist Terry Mattingly reported. "It was time for a prayer meeting. According to Lantz, at least fifty truckers and a slew of other drivers got together—a mere twenty miles from that Myersville rest area."[4]

Lantz later joked, "My wife asked me what I would've done if they had shot me. I replied, 'I don't know, but I'm going to heaven anyway.'"[5]

FAITH OF A CHILD

More than eight hundred volunteers were involved in the 2001 Easter pageant at our church. Each one was asked to pray for an unchurched person he or she hoped would come to see the pageant. Preaching Associate Dave Stone's nine-year-old daughter, Sadie, had a part in the pageant and decided to pray for a certain neighbor. But Dave was concerned. *I wish Sadie hadn't picked her*, he thought. *She'll just be disappointed. There's no way that lady will come.* Some ominous hurdles stood in the way. She was going through a divorce, which in this case seemed to be taking her further from God instead of closer to him. And for some reason she felt some animosity toward our fellowship; so even if she did decide to go to a church, it probably wouldn't be ours.

Sadie didn't contact the woman—she just prayed. A week before the pageant, out of the blue, the woman called and asked to talk with Dave. She had never called before, and Dave wondered what she wanted. "I just need to talk to you," she said. She expressed her desire to make things right with her husband. Dave talked to the couple for two hours the next day and helped them begin to put their relationship back together. Later the woman confided, "I don't know why I called you."

"I think I know why," Dave said. "My nine-year-old daughter, Sadie, has been praying for you to come to the Easter pageant!"

Dave didn't tell Sadie anything about the woman's call or the subsequent counseling session. He shared later:

The last night of the program, she and her husband came. I hadn't told Sadie anything about it. She came up and found Sadie afterward. I said, "Sadie, there's somebody here to see you." I wish you could have seen Sadie's face! She just kept saying over and over to the woman, "Thank you so much for coming! Thank you so much for coming!" and the woman kept saying, "Oh, no—thank you for praying!"

...AND MANY OTHERS

Shirley Taylor cried to God for a break. Keeping her four young children and her father-in-law, who was unable to care for himself, was exhausting, and she literally begged God for the chance to go out to dinner with her husband. "McDonald's—even White Castle would have been fine," she said. Her husband came home from work a couple of days later and said his manager had told him to do a little more entertaining with his clients—and to be sure to include his wife. Not only was Shirley given some badly needed evenings away at some really nice restaurants, but the business even paid for their meals and the baby-sitter!

❦

Elizabeth Jeffries prayed earnestly for her twenty-two-year-old nephew, Brian, who had been immersed in drugs and alcohol since he was fourteen. One holiday Brian was sent to yet another treatment center, and again the family earnestly prayed for him. Elizabeth prayed that God would send someone into his life who could show him Jesus. A few months later, Brian called to say that he had found a church he liked and that he had decided to give his burden to Jesus and be baptized. "I'm born again," he said.

The story is bittersweet. Brian's treatment was successful, and he was released from the treatment center. But two days later he suffered cardiac arrest and died. Elizabeth wrote, "The pain of losing this special young man was only softened by the joy of knowing that he now rests in the arms of our Savior, free at last from all addictions."

℘

Chris and Debbie Carper couldn't decide how much money to commit to the capital campaign for our church's new sanctuary. During a worship service Debbie prayed, "Lord, please show Chris and me what you want us to do." Uncharacteristically, she felt as if God was telling her exactly the amount they should give.

When they got home she said, "Chris, I feel like God told me how much we're supposed to give to the capital campaign."

"What did he say?" Chris asked.

Debbie was a little afraid to tell him, so she said, "You tell me!"

Chris blurted out the exact amount she had been thinking. "I feel like God spoke to me today too," he said.

℘

After fourteen years of marriage, the wife of a man in our church decided she couldn't love him anymore and that she was leaving. He begged God to forgive him for his failures as a husband and to restore their marriage. One day, after several weeks of separation, the man was sitting in church when he glanced to his left, and there in the aisle was his wife! He invited her to join him, and she did. "I felt God's power and presence that day and knew he was involved in saving our marriage," the man said. The two were later reunited and, shortly thereafter, were baptized at Southeast. "The Lord continues to bless us," he said. "God is awesome."

℘

In the first few minutes after Robert Taylor's wife underwent extensive surgery, the IV in her arm became dislodged. A couple of nurses tried unsuccessfully to reinsert the needle so she could get the critical medicinal fluid. Their frustration turned to desperation as each attempt failed. Finally, a burly nurse with seniority was called in. She sat quietly and held Sue's arm without moving or saying anything for about thirty seconds. Then she picked up the needle and immediately inserted it correctly on her first attempt. One of the nurses asked for an explanation of the half-minute pause. She said she had learned years ago that what we cannot do alone, we can do with God's help. In so many words, she said, "I prayed! You ought to try it too!"

℘

When Sandy Gootee told her mother she had become a Christian, her mother got angry and accused her of being a fanatic. For two years the woman wouldn't even speak to her daughter, but Sandy prayed that her mother would someday find Christ. Shortly after the death of Sandy's father, her mother became ill and was hospitalized. She called Sandy early one morning to let her know that she had been praying and reading the Bible all night and had given her life to Christ. The chaplain had come in and baptized her in the middle of the night. A day later, the woman got better and went home, but within twenty-four hours, she became ill again and died. "But praise Jesus," Sandy said, "she is now with him. I and many people had prayed daily for her. It works."

℘

When Andrea Williams was ten years old, her mother told her and her seven-year-old sister about the power of prayer. Her mother quoted Matthew 18:19: "If two of you on earth agree about anything you ask for, it will be done for you by my Father in heaven." Andrea and her sister decided to test that verse in a dramatic way. They knew a man—Paul Schieber—who had been blind for more than twenty years. They prayed that God would give their friend his sight. Five years later, after nearly thirty years of blindness, Paul Schieber underwent surgery and received his sight. Andrea admitted that the answered prayer gave her confidence in God's faithfulness. Since then, she said, "He has answered so many big prayers in my life, it's hard to keep track!"

℘

Bob Larsson, director of Pinehaven Christian Children's Ranch in Montana, tells of a time when finances were tight but they desperately needed a well for their church camp in a remote northwest section of the state. They were told that a well on the other side of the lake had been brought in at eight hundred feet, and still the water was unusable. But they knew they had to try. The consultant said it would cost at least ten thousand dollars to dig even three hundred feet. The amount was staggering for the small ministry, but they stepped out in faith. Bob stood by as the well diggers began their work. After three hours of drilling, they hit the perfect type of water—from a strata of fractured rock—at only seventy feet, producing thirty gallons of water a minute!

℘

In 1982, Karen lived with her husband and six-month-old son in Nashville when her husband was diagnosed with lung cancer. It was a shock, since he was a nonsmoker in good health. His family and their church in Nashville prayed for him, and the church leaders laid their hands on him and prayed. In spite of this, Karen's husband passed away seven months later at the age of twenty-eight. (Not all of our prayers are answered affirmatively. We'll discuss that more in the next section.)

A year later Karen moved to Louisville, Kentucky, with her son in order to be near her parents and try to rebuild her life. When Karen's former in-laws came to visit her and their grandson a few months later, they told her they had begun praying specifically for a husband for her and a father for Jordan. Karen wrote, "They began to ask God to send someone who is a Christian, has never been married before or has any other children, doesn't drink or smoke, and is financially stable. How about that for a wish list?"

Within two months, Karen met her future husband, Ken Brown. "He was twenty-nine, never married, a strong believer, didn't smoke or drink, was an up-and-coming and successful architect, and he was handsome on top of that!" she reported. A year later they were married. Ken adopted Jordan with the blessing of Karen's former in-laws. Jordan is now twenty years old, thankful to have a good adoptive father, and looking forward to a reunion in heaven with his biological dad someday.

℘

Husen Amanov was a Ukrainian man with a grotesque tumor on the side of his head that caused his enlarged ear to hang down near his shoulder. Charles and Penny Faust, from our church, faithfully prayed for him and brought him to America, hoping to raise enough money for surgery. We asked him to stand up before our congregation, and we prayed for his healing. The money needed to pay for his surgery—$121,000—was raised.

Without the extensive and risky operation, Husen had very little time to live. But the surgery was successful, and Husen returned home. I recently saw a picture of him—he has completely recovered and looks great! He now ministers to children in his home church and community. In a country where people believed he had been cursed by their god, he is telling about the grace of the one true God.

℘

There are many more stories of dramatic answers to prayer that I don't have time or space to recount here. Magda from Poland told about a time God provided her with shoes for the winter so she could go to the Christian camp she wanted to attend. Brook Brotzman told of the dramatic way God provided ten thousand dollars for a van their mission needed. Pam Veith mentioned the year when finances were tight and someone donated tuition money for her teenager's schooling. Dennis wrote about the way God intervened and brought healing when his wife was critically ill. Many others wrote about God's answering prayers for physical healing, financial provision, salvation of those who seemed beyond hope, protection in danger, comfort in grief, a friend in a time of loneliness, and on and on. God does answer prayer, and sometimes he does it in dramatic fashion.

THE LESSON TO BE LEARNED

Certainly, a lot of people could have written about unanswered prayers. Questions abound as to why God chooses to answer some prayers dramatically and not others. We'll address some of those questions in the next section; but for now, I want to impress upon you this one truth: At least on occasion, God still intervenes dramatically in the affairs of mankind.

> I've dreamed many dreams that never came true;
> I've seen them vanish at dawn.
> But I've realized enough of my dreams, thank God,
> To make me want to dream on.
> I've prayed many prayers when no answer came
> Though I waited patient and long.
> But answers have come to enough of my prayers
> To keep me praying on.[6]

Chapter Six

WHEN SHOULD WE PRAY FOR DRAMATIC ANSWERS?

*Every great movement of God can be
traced to a kneeling figure.*
—Dwight L. Moody

Just days before he was supposed to move to Kentucky and join our staff, Kyle Idleman was at home in southern California. He walked into the bedroom of his two-year-old daughter, Morgan, to wake her from a nap. He was singing as he opened the door, trying to awaken her as gently as possible. To his horror, he saw that her five-foot-tall chest of drawers had fallen over, and there was no sign of Morgan. In a panic, he screamed for his wife and lifted the chest of drawers. There lay Morgan—unconscious, black and blue, and already showing several large bumps on her head. "We called 911," Kyle said. "It just rang and rang. It must have rung twenty times before I scooped Morgan up in my arms and sped to the hospital with my wife."

As Kyle's wife, Desiree, held Morgan—still unconscious—in the backseat, Kyle continued trying desperately to call 911. Still no one responded. "While waiting for an answer, I listened as my wife prayed out loud for our daughter," Kyle said. "I finally hung up the phone and began praying with her."

At the hospital, they were bombarded with doctors and nurses. Morgan had sustained nerve damage, which at first doctors feared would be permanent; she could be paralyzed. Kyle's father, Ken Idleman, a longtime friend of mine, called to tell us of the accident. Scores of people from California to Kentucky began praying for Morgan. After myriad tests, doctors found that the only serious nerve damage was in her left leg, which was still paralyzed. They believed that the nerve would heal itself and that Morgan would be able to move her leg within six months, but they feared that in the meantime, palsy might set in and cause long-term damage. Kyle shared:

> Every morning for the next several days, my wife and I would go in and pray for her and then ask her to move her toes. She would stare at her toes and then smile at us and say, "They don't work!" Then one morning, after we prayed, we said, "Morgan, move your toes." And she did. They moved—just a little. But they moved.

Today Morgan is doing well and seems to have suffered no permanent damage. Reflecting on the event, Kyle concluded, "The only time in my life I called 911, no one answered. But God was there for us when we needed him the most."

The psalmist wrote, "When I was in distress, I sought the LORD" (Psalm 77:2). Do you pray in times of trouble? When your teacher says, "There will be a pop quiz today," do you pray, "Oh Lord, come quickly"? When you discover a strange lump on your body, do you immediately pray, "Oh

God, please don't let it be cancerous, and give me the strength to trust you"? When your employer says, "I'd like to meet with you tomorrow at eleven o'clock," do you pray, "Lord, keep my job secure"? When you slip on an icy road, do you pray, "Lord, help me get this vehicle under control"? When you discover a chest of drawers has fallen on your child, do you pray, "Lord, help her, let her be OK, and keep us strong"?

James wrote, "Is any one of you in trouble? He should pray" (James 5:13). You might be thinking, *That's not a problem! Doesn't everyone pray when they're in trouble?* Not necessarily. A lot of people don't turn to the Lord even in the middle of a great crisis. Federal aviation inspectors say that when they listen to the final words of airline pilots just before a crash, they frequently hear profanity. The very last words recorded on tape and preserved in the black box often are not prayers but curses.

ARE YOU PREPARED TO PRAY WHEN TROUBLE STRIKES?

God expects you to call on him when you're in trouble. You might say to your children, "If you have any trouble, stop and call me." You want them to rely on you when they're in a crisis; your heavenly Father wants you to rely on him when you're in a crisis. So why don't people instinctively pray when they're in trouble?

If you don't turn to God when tragedy strikes, it's probably one of two reasons: Either you don't believe he can help, so you just don't ask (as we discussed in chapter 3); or you're not in the habit of going to him under normal circumstances, so when the pressure is on, you do whatever it is you normally do.

When faced with severe trouble, people instinctively revert back to lifelong habits. That's why the recording caught the pilots cursing God instead of praying to him. That was their habit. Whether you pray in times of trouble will depend on your daily routine. If you're not going to God on a daily basis for strength and guidance, it's not likely you'll turn to him in a crisis. Like those pilots, you'll revert to your habits when trouble strikes. If your routine is more characterized by cursing than praying, you'll be more likely to curse God than to pray to him even in your darkest hour.

A good basketball player practices free throws over and over, shooting them exactly the same way. He hopes to develop such good habits that when the pressure is on, he can still perform well. He knows that in stressful situations, the body responds as it has been trained to respond. So do the mind and the spirit.

Luke 22:44 describes Jesus' prayer in Gethsemane just hours before his crucifixion: "Being in anguish, he prayed more earnestly, and his sweat was like drops of blood falling to the ground." In Christ's darkest hour, he prayed. His prayer may have been more intense than usual, but it was natural for him to turn to his father for help because that's what he was used to doing. The Bible says that during Jesus' busy days, when the crowds were following him and everything was going well, he "often withdrew to lonely places and prayed" (Luke 5:16).

When our children were toddlers, my wife and I developed a habit of reading a Bible story to them and praying with them before they went to sleep. We faithfully went through that routine each night. Sometimes it seemed like we were just going through the motions, but it was an acknowledgment that God was real to us and that prayer was a vital part of every day. As the children grew older, we usually gathered around the kitchen table late in the evening for a few minutes before they went off to bed. One of us would read a section of Scripture, and then both boys would take turns praying aloud.

A few years later, we went through one of those periods of teenage rebellion. I discovered that one of my sons had violated a family rule in a major way, and I was angry. When I confronted him, he confessed and apologized. He could tell he had wounded me, and he broke down and wept. His tears broke my heart. I put my arms around him and held him like I did when he was a little child. He sobbed, "Dad, could we pray or something?" We knelt by the couch and prayed. It was a heartwarming, cleansing moment that bound us together. But it never would have happened—it never would have been so natural for my son to want to pray with me—if many years earlier we hadn't developed the sometimes-perfunctory habit of praying together each night.

When you are going to God daily for strength and wisdom, you will more naturally turn to him when tragedy strikes.

DO YOU PRAY FOR OTHER CHRISTIANS IN TROUBLE?

The Bible commands us to "always keep on praying for all the saints" (Ephesians 6:18). You might go to God when you're in trouble, and you might pray for those close to you when they're in trouble. But those of us in America often overlook a large group of saints facing daily trouble: the persecuted Christians. The Hebrew writer urged, "Remember those in prison as if you were their fellow prisoners, and those who are mistreated as if you yourselves were suffering" (Hebrews 13:3).

THE PERSECUTED CHURCH

Paul Marshall, in his book *Their Blood Cries Out*, exposed the tragic injustices being meted out against Christians in many countries today. A summary of the book reads:

> In Sudan, Christians are enslaved. In Iran, they are assassinated. In Cuba, they are imprisoned. In China, they are beaten to death. In more than sixty countries worldwide, Christians are harassed, abused, arrested, tortured, or executed specifically because of their faith. 200,000,000 Christians throughout the world live in daily fear of secret police, vigilantes, or state repression or discrimination. These are not wild rumors. Nor are they simply Christians who, like many others, suffer from war or tyranny. Hundreds of millions of Christians are suffering simply because of what they believe.[1]

Each year more than 150,000 Christians are killed for their faith.[2] That's more than were being killed by the

Roman Empire in the first three centuries, when we imag-ine persecution being at its worst. The fact is that more Christians died for their faith in the last century than in the first nineteen centuries *combined*.³

Christian musicians dc talk recently published a revised version of the old *Foxe's Book of Martyrs*, entitled *Jesus Freaks*. The book contains several modern-day accounts of the persecution and martyrdom many Christians have courageously endured in countries dominated by commu-nists and Muslims.

The book recounts the courageous story of Pastor Kim and his flock of twenty-seven Christians in North Korea. They lived in hand-dug tunnels for a number of years, hiding from the hostile communist government. But when government officials built a road through that area, the underground community was discovered. The officials brought them out before a crowd of thirty thousand in the village of Gok San for a public trial and execution. The Christians were told, "Deny Christ or die." When they refused, four children were seized from the group and pre-pared for hanging. With ropes tied around their tiny necks, the merciless officer again commanded the parents of the children to deny Christ. They told their children, "We will see you in heaven," and the children died quietly.

As if that were not barbaric enough, the officer then called for a steamroller and forced the believers to lie down in its path. As the engine revved, the church members were given one last chance to recant. Again they refused.

Together the Christians began to sing a hymn as the steamroller inched forward:

> More love to thee, O Christ, more love to Thee
> Thee alone I seek, more love to Thee
> Let sorrow do its work, more love to Thee
> Then shall my latest breath whisper thy praise
> This be the parting cry my heart shall raise;
> More love, O Christ, to Thee.[4]

The North Korean press reported the execution as an effort to suppress superstition.[5]

Persecution of Christians is a fact of daily life not only in North Korea but also in Cuba, Iran, Vietnam, China, Sudan, Pakistan, Saudi Arabia, and many other nations around the world. We ought to be doing whatever we can to assist these brothers and sisters in Christ. We are commanded, "Speak up for those who cannot speak for themselves, for the rights of all who are destitute. Speak up and judge fairly; defend the rights of the poor and needy" (Proverbs 31:8–9). The Bible says:

> Rescue those being led away to death; hold back those staggering toward slaughter. If you say, "But we knew nothing about this," does not he who weighs the heart perceive it? Does not he who guards your life know it? Will he not repay each person according to what he has done? (Proverbs 24:11–12)

Thankfully even some non-Christians like columnist Michael Horowitz have begun to petition the American government to open their eyes to the atrocities being conducted against Christians around the world. If these happenings are appalling even to those who do not share our faith, how much more should they break our hearts?

At the very least, we should be praying for the persecuted church. It's only natural that we pray for protection and freedom for those who are suffering. But is that all?

Acts 4 tells us that Peter and John were arrested and imprisoned for preaching that Jesus of Nazareth had risen from the dead. The next day they were released, but the religious leaders who arrested them warned them not to preach about Jesus again. Peter and John responded boldly: "Judge for yourselves whether it is right in God's sight to obey you rather than God. For we cannot help speaking about what we have seen and heard" (Acts 4:19–20). Then they went to the Christian community and reported all that had been done to them and the threats against them. When the believers heard what had happened, "they raised their voices together in prayer to God" (Acts 4:24).

The Early Church sensed the pressure these men were under, so they met to pray. You might imagine that they would pray for relief from persecution. Instead, they prayed, "Lord, consider their threats and enable your servants to speak your word with great boldness" (Acts 4:29). They prayed not for freedom or protection but for boldness! The Bible says, "After they prayed, the place where they were meeting was shaken. And they were all filled with the Holy Spirit and spoke the word of God boldly" (Acts 4:31). They prayed for boldness, and God gave them boldness! And he gave them the opportunity to use their courage to the glory of Jesus Christ.

So when you pray for the persecuted church, don't just pray that God will protect them. Pray that they will remain faithful and proclaim boldly the gospel of Jesus Christ.

TROUBLE CHRISTIANS FACE IN AMERICA

Christians in America rarely face arrest, imprisonment, or death. We face lawsuits, labels, political correctness, loss of tax exemption, media gibes, and derision from the intellectual elite.

For example, a developer in our city paid for an advertisement in a local newspaper. The ad promoted his new housing project and noted that it was "near Southeast Christian Church." An executive from the Fairness in Housing Commission called him to insist that he not repeat the advertisement, because it was discriminatory against non-Christians. The developer was threatened with a lawsuit if he didn't comply.

We need to pray that God will give us courage when facing such opposition. If our brothers and sisters in other countries can stand up for their faith when threatened with nooses and steamrollers, surely we can refuse to cower when faced with lawsuits and letters to the editor.

One of the graduating seniors in our church was asked to give the benediction at the end of her baccalaureate service. She was warned that it was to be an "inspirational moment," and she was cautioned not to pray. Because the ACLU puts pressure on schools at graduation time, school attorneys often send out memos to principals saying things like, "If at all possible, please instruct your students not to pray. Instruct them to say something meaningful or to read something inspirational. If they insist on having a time of prayer, make it a moment of silence." The ACLU is powerful because too many people cower to the opposition. We're terrified of legal entanglement. We fear the financial impact or the bad publicity such trouble can bring. We should be praying for the kind of boldness for which our brothers and sisters in other parts of the world are famous.

Sometimes when I'm preparing a sermon, I'll be studying a scripture or topic that brings to mind a "controversial" issue. I will sense the Holy Spirit leading me to deal with the issue from a biblical perspective. It might be the topic of abortion, homosexuality, divorce, women's roles in the church, the exclusive claims of Christ as the only way to salvation, or any of the dozens of other controversial subjects. I'm often tempted to think, *I don't want to appear anti-intellectual. I don't want the media ridiculing me. I don't want to make another pro-choice political candidate mad at me. I think I'll just avoid this topic. I'll skirt this issue.* A voice in my head will whisper, *Don't call it a perversion—call it a struggle. Don't tell them about divorce, tithing, or abstinence—those are old-fashioned ideas. Don't call it sin—call it "morally challenged." You don't want to offend anybody.*

But then I remember that I'm commissioned by God, through the Scripture, to preach the Word and to speak the truth in love—not just to say what itching ears want to hear.

I remember what one ambassador for Christ said even from a prison cell:

> Pray also for me, that whenever I open my mouth, words may be given me so that I will fearlessly make known the mystery of the gospel, for which I am an ambassador in chains. Pray that I may declare it fearlessly, as I should. (Ephesians 6:19–20)

I hope you will pray for me—and for other Christians who have the opportunity to speak up for Christ—that we may be able to proclaim the Word of Christ boldly and clearly.

DO YOU PRAY FOR A NATION IN TROUBLE?

God sent Jonah to warn the city of Nineveh of impending doom if they didn't repent of their wickedness. Rather than scoff at the threat of judgment, the city in trouble prayed. The king of Nineveh sent out the following decree:

> Do not let any man or beast, herd or flock, taste anything; do not let them eat or drink. But let man and beast be covered with sackcloth. Let everyone call urgently on God. Let them give up their evil ways and their violence. Who knows? God may yet relent and with compassion turn from his fierce anger so that we will not perish. (Jonah 3:7–9)

Their prayers were heard. God did relent and with compassion forgave the city of Nineveh. When our nation is in trouble, God's people need to pray.

AMERICA'S PRAYER OF REPENTANCE

Former governor of Kentucky Brereton Jones asked me to speak at the Governor's Prayer Breakfast during his final year in office in 1995. In my speech, I mentioned that our nation has turned away from God. We've lost our spiritual bearings, I said, and we need to repent. I wrote a prayer and suggested that we offer it as a nation:

O God, we know that your Word says, "Woe to those who call evil good," but that's exactly what we've done. We have lost our spiritual equilibrium and inverted our values.

We confess that we have ridiculed the absolute truth of your Word and called it moral pluralism.

We have worshipped other gods and called it multiculturalism and New Age spirituality.

We have committed adultery and called it an affair.

We have endorsed perversion and called it an alternative lifestyle.

We have exploited the poor and called it the lottery.

We have neglected the needy and called it frugality.

We have rewarded laziness and called it welfare.

We have killed our unborn children and called it choice.

We have shot abortionists and called it justifiable.

We have neglected to discipline our children and called it building self-esteem.

We have failed to execute justice speedily, as your Word commands, and called it due process.

We have failed to love our neighbor who has a different color of skin and called it maintaining racial purity.

We have abused power and called it political savvy.

We have coveted our neighbor's possessions and called it ambition.

We have polluted the air with profanity and pornography and called it freedom of expression.

We have made the Lord's Day the biggest shopping and entertainment day of the week and called it free enterprise.

We have ridiculed the time-honored values of our parents and called it enlightenment.

Search us, O God, and know our hearts today. Try us and see if there be some wicked way in us; cleanse us of every sin and set us free. Though our sins be as scarlet, may they become white as snow. Though they be as crimson, may they be as wool.[6]

A few months later I printed the prayer in my weekly column of the *Lookout Magazine.* My friend Joe Wright, pastor at Central Christian Church in Wichita, Kansas, read the prayer and was moved by it. He was scheduled to deliver the opening prayer before the Kansas House of Representatives two months later. On January 23, 1996, Joe Wright stood before those legislators and prayed that prayer! You may have heard about the controversy stirred that day. The prayer infuriated several legislators; one member stormed out of the hall in protest. Several gave speeches critical of the prayer, and one even called it a "message of intolerance."

Joe's staff stopped counting how many phone calls they received after the first sixty-five hundred. All but a small handful of the calls were supportive. Since then the church has been contacted by people from every state and many foreign countries asking for a copy of the prayer. I understand that the chaplain coordinator in the Nebraska legislature read the prayer the following month, stirring a debate there. Paul Harvey reported on the Kansas controversy and read the prayer on the air. He has since repeated the story, claiming it is one of the most requested readings he has ever had. The prayer has been widely circulated by e-mail. One of our elders recently sent it to me and said, "You need to read this prayer—it's great!"

Joe Wright and I have joked often about the publicity he received for the prayer I wrote. But it's OK with me—I didn't have to take all those hits! And he deserves credit for having the boldness to actually *pray* the prayer in front of the legislature! I'm thankful that this prayer has resonated with so many Americans. I hope we don't just read it but really pray it and genuinely repent before God.

A HISTORY OF PRAYER

One of the reasons the United States has been so blessed by God is that in times of trouble, leaders and citizens of this nation have always turned to prayer. The pilgrims barely survived the first winter in the new land. But they prayed that God would provide, and they made it through. When the first harvest came, they set aside a special time to thank God for his blessings.

George Washington knelt in the snow at Valley Forge and asked God for the resources needed for the Revolutionary army to survive. Against all odds, they survived and defeated the most powerful army in the world to gain their independence.

When the Constitutional Convention met in 1787,

tempers flared and harsh words were spoken in the debate over how the new government should operate. After much argument, the members had come to a stalemate. But Benjamin Franklin, aged and ailing, made yet one more important contribution to the young nation—he asked for God's intervention. "God governs in the affairs of men," he said, addressing George Washington and the assembly. "And if a sparrow cannot fall to the ground without his notice, is it probable that an empire can rise without his aid?" Franklin then suggested beginning each session with prayer and that a member of the clergy be retained to lead them in their supplications. Not only did this bring the Convention back to an essential focus, but it also led to the establishment of a chaplaincy in the United States Congress that remains to this day.[7]

Abraham Lincoln, perhaps the greatest president of our country, said, "I have been driven to my knees many times by the overwhelming conviction that I had no place else to go. My own wisdom and that of those about me seemed insufficient for the day."

The events of September 11, 2001, were tragic, but they resulted in a brief spiritual revival in America. As Max Lucado said, "Some evil men sought to drive America to her knees that fateful day, but they did not know the God to whom we pray when we are on our knees." Americans flocked to churches the evening of September 11 and in the days that followed, falling on their knees before God in prayer. The leaders of our nation openly called upon us to pray to God for America. For several months, the song "God Bless America" was, for all practical purposes, our national anthem. It was sung at every public gathering alongside the traditional "Star Spangled Banner," often with more zeal and enthusiasm.

THE FUTURE OF AMERICA

As we face an uncertain future with war and the threat of more terrorism always looming, we would be wise to pray, "Lord, help us avoid war if possible, but always to have the courage to stand for what is right. Protect our sons and daughters and allow justice to prevail. Lord, help us to repent of our immorality, greed, and disrespect for life, and may our nation turn to you."

I hear some Christian people talking pessimistically about America's future. "We're finished," they say. "We're a post-Christian nation now, and God will judge us for our disobedience." I agree that God will judge us if we do not repent, but we don't know the future. Our God is an awesome God, and he promises to listen to the prayers of his people. Jesus said, "With God all things are possible" (Matthew 19:26).

Who would have thought that communism would fall in the Soviet Union? One of the two most powerful nations in the world came unraveled. The Berlin Wall came tumbling down. What happened? Was it economic pressure? Did Gorbachev underestimate the power of reformation? One factor often overlooked is the faithful prayers of persecuted

Christians in Poland, Czechoslovakia, Ukraine, and other communist countries.

Chuck Colson, in his book *A Dance with Deception*, tells about visiting some Soviet prisons in 1990, just prior to the collapse of communism. He met a physicist named Alexander Goldovich, who had been arrested for trying to escape the USSR in a rowboat. Goldovich was sentenced to fifteen years of hard labor in a Siberian prison camp.

The KGB insisted on filming Colson's interview, but Colson said Goldovich still looked straight into the camera and fearlessly described his years of unjust torture in the prison camp. Colson said he couldn't help but admire the man's courage. Then he saw the source of his strength: Over in the corner, above the door, etched in the concrete, was a cross—a symbol of the spiritual power that had sustained him. It wasn't Gorbachev who changed the nation—it was men like Alexander Goldovich who were living righteous lives and praying for freedom.

Only time will tell whether America will return to her proud ways or continue to humble herself before God in times of trouble. The Bible says that the burden rests on those of us who call ourselves God's children. It's our job to take the lead in prayer. When we do, we have God's promise:

> If my people, who are called by my name, will humble themselves and pray and seek my face and turn from their wicked ways, then will I hear from heaven and will forgive their sin and will heal their land. (2 Chronicles 7:14)

Part Three

GOD
ANSWERS
PRAYER
DRAMATICALLY,
BUT NOT VERY OFTEN

Chapter Seven

WHY DIDN'T GOD ANSWER?

You have covered yourself with a cloud
so that no prayer can get through.
—Lamentations 3:44

A young woman wrote to me about the dramatic peace God provided for her in the midst of a terrifying experience:

> On May 11, 2001, I survived the attack of a serial rapist in the Lyndon area of Louisville. There were moments during those awful hours when I was held hostage that I told God that I was ready to come home if he was ready to take me there. When the perpetrator told me that we were leaving my home and going to ATM machines (where I was robbed), I suddenly accepted the fact that I would be dead within hours or even minutes. I simply prayed that God would protect my son and my family during their grief.
>
> As we got into the car, I had a gun poking in my side and a man yelling obscenities that made no sense. I concentrated on turning the key and following his demands. As I did so, I heard something profound. I heard the joyful noise of Southeast's worship team. I faithfully listened to the worship music CD in my car as I drove around each day. But as I sat in the driver's seat with a gun in my side and a masked assailant sitting next to me shouting,

I heard song number seven: "A Mighty Fortress Is Our God." At this moment, I had a gentle reminder that no matter what happened in the next few hours, I could seek refuge in him. I did. And I continue to do so. By the grace of God, I survived. And by the grace of God, I will use this experience to praise him.

When I first read that letter, I thought, *That's a great example of dramatic answer to prayer.* But as I pondered the story some more, another thought came to mind: *Why didn't God answer her prayer for protection?* I'm thankful her life was spared, but why wasn't she spared from the physical attack and the terrible trauma that followed?

Why doesn't God answer all of our prayers?

The movie *Signs* starred Mel Gibson as an Anglican priest whose wife was hit and killed by an automobile. The priest was so angry at God for letting his wife die that he became an atheist and left the ministry. If God really cares for us, why doesn't he prove it by responding affirmatively to our simplest requests? For those of us who believe in a holy, loving, just, prayer-answering God, that's a tough question to answer.

Jeremiah complained, "You have covered yourself with a cloud so that no prayer can get through" (Lamentations 3:44). Have you felt that way sometimes? I have! I've prayed that God would spare the life of a child battling leukemia, and the child still died. I've prayed for God to keep a marriage together through a difficult time, and the

132

couple still got divorced. I've prayed for relief from stress, and more responsibility came. I recently prayed that the baby developing in the womb of my daughter-in-law Lisa would be healthy; but she had a miscarriage—her third in a year. You could probably add some of your own unanswered prayers to this list. Why didn't God answer your prayer? And what should your reaction be when God seems to be silent, hidden behind the clouds?

LACK OF FAITH

The Bible indicates that there is a direct link between faith and answered prayer. The Book of James says:

> If any of you lacks wisdom, he should ask God, who gives generously to all without finding fault, and it will be given to him. But when he asks, he must believe and not doubt, because he who doubts is like a wave of the sea, blown and tossed by the wind. That man should not think he will receive anything from the Lord; he is a double-minded man, unstable in all he does. (James 1:5–8)

Jesus often chastised people for having too little faith. He said that if we just had faith the size of a mustard seed, we could move mountains (see Matthew 17:20). What exactly does that mean? When my request is denied, am I to assume that God is refusing to answer my prayer because I don't have enough faith? To help answer that question, let's consider two men of faith who didn't get all their prayers answered affirmatively.

133

MOSES AND THE PROMISED LAND

God had told Moses he would not be crossing over with the children of Israel into the Promised Land because of his recent indiscretion. But as Moses' life neared its end, he was hoping God would just let him go over and take a peek. Maybe God would temporarily suspend his sentence or at least let him out on parole for the weekend. Moses later told the Israelites,

> I pleaded with the LORD: "O Sovereign LORD, you have begun to show to your servant your greatness and your strong hand. For what god is there in heaven or on earth who can do the deeds and mighty works you do? Let me go over and see the good land beyond the Jordan." (Deuteronomy 3:23–25)

You might remember why Moses was being denied this request. God had taken care of him and the Israelites for forty years as they wandered in the wilderness. Shortly before they were to enter the Promised Land, God led them to the Desert of Zin, where they ran out of water—again. And as their parents had done forty years earlier, the children of Israel complained and grumbled against their leaders. They organized an official protest and demanded an explanation from Moses and Aaron.

God told Moses to speak to the rock in front of him, and the rock would bring forth plenty of water for the Israelites to drink. But when Moses gathered the people together, forty years of frustration with this obstinate, faithless group boiled up within him. Instead of speaking to the rock as

God had commanded, Moses yelled at the people: "Listen, you rebels, must we bring you water out of this rock" for you to believe (Numbers 20:10)? Moses vented his anger by flailing away at the rock with his staff. Water gushed out, and the people and the livestock had plenty to drink.

But God had not said to strike the rock; he had said to speak to the rock, and God was not pleased with Moses' disobedience.

I can understand Moses. His sister, Miriam, had just died, and he was emotionally drained. The ongoing murmuring of these petty, ungrateful, doubting people just got under his skin. He had reached the limit of his tolerance. He was completely exasperated with them.

Still, Moses' loss of temper brought a stern rebuke from God. Actually, Moses had battled this particular character flaw all of his life. When he was forty years old, his anger had driven him to kill an Egyptian taskmaster who was beating a Hebrew slave. When Moses was eighty, he came down off Mount Sinai to find the children of Israel worshiping a golden calf. In a rage, he hurled down the brand-new stone tablets on which God had etched the Ten Commandments and smashed them on the rocks below. Now, at the end of his life, he again found himself in trouble because of his temper.

God, in his holiness, was offended by this rash action. Moses had not shown proper respect for God in front of God's people. The New Testament tells us that the rock represented Christ himself (see 1 Corinthians 10:4). It's possible that

God's intention was for the rock to be struck only one time, as he had commanded forty years ago—as a symbol that his Son would only have to be struck once for all the sins of the people. This second striking of the rock ruined the symbol, was disobedient, and was disrespectful of the holy rock God had provided. So the Lord said to Moses, "Because you have disobeyed me, you will not be permitted to go over into the Promised Land" (see Numbers 20:12).

Even considering all the possible symbolism, that's still a pretty harsh judgment. You can understand why, a few weeks later, Moses begged God to reconsider. It seemed like a reasonable request. Moses had sacrificed forty years of his life for this cause, and he hadn't even wanted the job. Now, finally, the Israelites were preparing to enter the land God had promised—the land described as "flowing with milk and honey"—and Moses simply asked, "Lord, can I please at least go over and see it?" If you were God, wouldn't you relent just a little? You'd say, "OK, Moses, you've been a faithful servant. I'll let you go over and scout it out." But God didn't answer Moses' prayer affirmatively.

PAUL'S THORN IN THE FLESH

The apostle Paul, in his second letter to the church at Corinth, wrote about a physical ailment he had:

> To keep me from becoming conceited because of these surpassingly great revelations, there was given me a thorn in my flesh, a messenger of Satan, to torment me.

Three times I pleaded with the Lord to take it away from me. (2 Corinthians 12:7–8)

Have you ever had a painful splinter you can't get out of your hand or foot? If Paul referred to his problem as a thorn, it must have been a daily, painful, irritating, nearly debilitating physical problem. No one knows exactly what Paul's thorn in the flesh was, but we can speculate. In his letter to the Galatians, Paul mentions an illness he had when he visited them:

> As you know, it was because of an illness that I first preached the gospel to you. Even though my illness was a trial to you, you did not treat me with contempt or scorn. Instead, you welcomed me as if I were an angel of God, as if I were Christ Jesus himself. (Galatians 4:13–14)

Paul later mentions how they were willing to tear out their own eyes to give to him, so the illness must have affected his eyesight. At the end of the same book he wrote, "See what large letters I use as I write to you with my own hand!" (Galatians 6:11).

Because of these passages, historians speculate that perhaps Paul contracted a severe illness while on his first missionary journey that affected his eyesight for the rest of his life. The illness may have even frequently recurred. So it might have been the illness itself or the waning eyesight to which Paul was referring as his thorn in the flesh.

Others have speculated that perhaps Paul had a speech

impediment that caused people to make fun of his lack of charisma when he preached. He told the Corinthians:

> When I came to you, brothers, I did not come with eloquence or superior wisdom as I proclaimed to you the testimony about God. For I resolved to know nothing while I was with you except Jesus Christ and him crucified. I came to you in weakness and fear, and with much trembling. My message and my preaching were not with wise and persuasive words, but with a demonstration of the Spirit's power, so that your faith might not rest on men's wisdom, but on God's power. (1 Corinthians 2:1–5)

It seems a little less likely that Paul would refer to a speech impediment as a thorn in the flesh. And Paul's point in 1 Corinthians is that it was the truthfulness of the message, not Paul's fancy rhetorical skills, that persuaded people to follow Christ. I'm more inclined to believe that Paul's thorn was something more physical, like an illness or debilitating eyesight. But all of this is speculation anyway. Whatever the thorn was, Paul was convinced that it limited his effectiveness, and it must have been a daily irritation to him. It bothered him so much that he prayed repeatedly that God would heal him.

From a human perspective, that seems like a reasonable request. Here's a man who has sacrificed all his ambitions for Christ. He has endured an incalculable amount of suffering for the sake of Christ. Paul himself described it:

> Five times I received from the Jews the forty lashes minus one. Three times I was beaten with rods, once I was stoned, three times I was shipwrecked, I spent a night

and a day in the open sea, I have been constantly on the move. I have been in danger from rivers, in danger from bandits, in danger from my own countrymen, in danger from Gentiles; in danger in the city, in danger in the country, in danger at sea; and in danger from false brothers. I have labored and toiled and have often gone without sleep; I have known hunger and thirst and have often gone without food; I have been cold and naked. Besides everything else, I face daily the pressure of my concern for all the churches. (2 Corinthians 11:24–28)

Paul's life was tough enough as it was. He didn't need additional problems. If anyone ever deserved to have a "thorn" removed, it was Paul. If you were God, wouldn't you grant his request and give him relief from the pain and embarrassment of the thorn in his flesh? After all, this is *the* apostle Paul—the greatest Christian who ever lived! Doesn't he deserve a little favored treatment?

But God said no. God told Paul he would have to live with his infirmity the rest of his life. "My grace is sufficient for you," God said to Paul, "for my power is made perfect in weakness" (2 Corinthians 12:9).

FAITH MISUNDERSTOOD

The Bible mentions many others besides Moses and Paul whose prayers were not always answered affirmatively. Abraham asked God to spare the cities of Sodom and Gomorrah, but they were still destroyed. Elijah was so depressed that he asked God to take his life, but God didn't. David fasted and prayed for a week, asking God to spare the life of his infant son who was ill, but the baby still died. Habakkuk prayed that his people would not be punished by the ruthless Babylonians, but they were. What, then, did James mean when he said a person who asks must "believe and not doubt"? What did Jesus mean when he said all we needed was a little faith to move mountains?

Some people think that any time we pray and don't get the answer we had hoped for, it's because we didn't have enough faith. There's a lot of false teaching to that effect today, which is causing unnecessary confusion and doubt. If it's true that anytime our prayers are unanswered, it's because we didn't have enough faith, then Moses, Paul, Abraham, Elijah, and the rest—and even Jesus—lacked faith.

Even the Son of God didn't get every prayer answered the way he wanted. Jesus prayed, Let this cup pass from me—nevertheless not my will but yours be done (see Matthew 26:39). So when James says we must "believe and not doubt," he doesn't mean we should be positive that our prayers will be answered just as we want. It would be arrogant of us to assume to know better than God how he should answer our prayers. Those who claim each of God's no answers is because of a lack of faith are ignoring the possibility that what we want could be to our own detriment. God's wisdom is higher than our wisdom.

THE KIND OF FAITH GOD WANTS

What kind of faith does God really want? Hebrews 11:6 tells us: "Without faith it is impossible to please God, because anyone who comes to him must believe that he exists and that he rewards those who earnestly seek him." Faith, then, means sincerely believing in two things: First, we must believe in God's presence. We must "believe that he exists." Faith means coming to God believing that he is real, that he is hearing your prayers, and that he has the power to do something about them. Second, we must believe in God's goodness. We must believe "that he rewards those who earnestly seek him" (Hebrews 11:6).

BELIEVING HE IS REAL

When Jesus went to Nazareth, the Bible says he couldn't do many miracles because of the people's lack of faith (see Matthew 13:58; Mark 6:5–6). What happened there? Did people come for healing and get turned away by Jesus because of their lack of faith? No—that's not what the Scriptures say. Unlike some modern faith healers, Jesus never turned away anyone who came to him for healing. Jesus wasn't excusing his inability to perform miracles by claiming the people must not have had enough faith. In fact, sometimes Jesus performed miracles when it seemed nobody believed at all—like the raising of the widow's son, the healing of the man with the withered hand, and the raising of Lazarus from the dead. So Jesus wasn't bound by the amount of faith of the person needing to be healed.

Why, then, could he not do many miracles in Nazareth? Because the people had so little faith in Jesus that they didn't even come to ask! He couldn't do miracles there because nobody was asking for them. That's why the Scripture says he couldn't do "many" miracles. A few came and received healing. But the crowds were small because most of the people lacked enough faith to even show up. They were so sure that Jesus wasn't anything special ("Isn't this the carpenter's son? Didn't we watch him grow up?") that they didn't even entertain the possibility that he could heal them.

In contrast, consider the account in Mark 9 of the father whose son was healed of a demon:

> A man in the crowd answered, "Teacher, I brought you my son, who is possessed by a spirit that has robbed him of speech. Whenever it seizes him, it throws him to the ground. He foams at the mouth, gnashes his teeth and becomes rigid. I asked your disciples to drive out the spirit, but they could not."
>
> "O unbelieving generation," Jesus replied, "how long shall I stay with you? How long shall I put up with you? Bring the boy to me."
>
> So they brought him. When the spirit saw Jesus, it immediately threw the boy into a convulsion. He fell to the ground and rolled around, foaming at the mouth.
>
> Jesus asked the boy's father, "How long has he been like this?"
>
> "From childhood," he answered. "It has often thrown him into fire or water to kill him. But if you can do anything, take pity on us and help us."
>
> "'If you can'?" said Jesus. "Everything is possible for him who believes."

Immediately the boy's father exclaimed, "I do believe; help me overcome my unbelief!" (Mark 9:17–24)

Jesus healed the boy[1] and counted the father as a believer, even though he had imperfect faith. How much faith does it take for Jesus to consider us to be praying "in faith"? How big is mustard-seed-sized faith? This passage leads me to believe that all we need is faith strong enough to sincerely offer the prayer. It has to be sincere belief. If you offend God by patronizing him when you really don't believe he exists, don't expect him to answer your prayer. But you can even be fighting genuine doubts and still have your prayer answered—if you have enough faith to ask.

So if God chooses not to answer your prayer, don't worry that it was because of your lack of faith. Only a hypocrite would pray to God for healing and have no faith at all that the prayer could be answered. Assuming you aren't just mouthing the words while your heart says, "I don't really believe in a God who can heal," you are praying in faith. As long as you are praying with a sincere heart, God will listen to your prayer. When you have doubts, pray, "Lord, I do believe. Help my unbelief!"

BELIEVING HE IS GOOD

The Hebrew writer said we must also "believe...that he rewards those who earnestly seek him" (Hebrews 11:6). A person praying with faith believes that God is good—that he has a righteous character and our best interests in mind.

A Gentile woman came to Jesus, desperate to get some help for her ailing daughter. Instead of healing the daughter right away, Jesus tested the mother by disparaging her race and acting as though he weren't going to heal her daughter. Jesus said, "It is not right to take the children's bread and toss it to their dogs" (Matthew 15:26). It would have been tempting for a Gentile to take offense at this comment and stomp off in a huff. But the woman was desperate. She decided to trust in the goodness of this man and respond humbly: "'Yes, Lord,' she said, 'but even the dogs eat the crumbs that fall from their masters' table'" (Matthew 15:27).

Jesus was pleased with the woman's response. "Woman, you have great faith!" he told her. "'Your request is granted.' And her daughter was healed from that very hour" (Matthew 15:28).

What did Jesus mean by "great faith"? What exactly was he testing? Her faith in his ability to heal? No—she had already proven that she believed he could heal, or she wouldn't have come. He was testing her faith *in his good character.* Did she truly believe he was good? Would her faith in him and in his character weaken if it appeared he wasn't going to heal her daughter as she had hoped? Jesus said she had "great faith" not because she believed more than others did in Jesus' healing power but because she trusted Jesus' goodness more than most would have under such a test.

144

God isn't just concerned with your faith in his ability to heal. When you come to him with a request, you're demonstrating that you believe he can honor that request. God is also concerned with your faith in his character. How will you respond if he says no? Will you still have faith? Will you still trust in his goodness even if you don't get your way? Do you really have faith in him not only to heal but to do what is right in all circumstances?

THE PRAYER OF FAITH

Faith, then, does not mean confidence that God will do exactly what we request. Faith is not believing that God *will* answer your prayers; it is believing that God *can* and *may*. When you pray, you must "believe and not doubt." What are you to believe? That God exists and that he is good. He hears your prayer, he cares about you, and he will respond according to what is best.

Suppose one of my grandchildren said to me, "Pop, I know you have the money, and I know what's best for me— I want a pet lion. I know if you really love me, you'll give me the lion." Will I conclude that they must have great faith in me? No, I'll conclude that they're manipulative, self-centered, and foolish. If we say to God, "Lord, this is what I want, and because I have so much faith, I'm going to believe you're going to give it to me," he will likely come to a similar conclusion.

What, then, does a prayer offered in faith sound like?

Let's say you're praying for a loved one who is ill, and you really want God to heal him or her. A prayer of faith might sound something like this:

Dear Father in heaven, I believe that you are the God who heals. I know you've healed people in the past. You healed King Hezekiah of his illness and gave him fifteen more years of life. You raised the widow's son through the prophet Elijah. You healed the blind, the deaf, and the lame through Jesus Christ and his apostles. You created this universe, and you know everything about it. You know my relative's body better than any doctor could ever know it, because you created it. You promised that the prayer of faith will make the sick person well, and I'm asking you to heal my loved one.

Yet, Lord, I also trust that your will is better than my will. And so I ask also for the strength to accept your will and to believe in your goodness no matter what you choose to do. If you choose to heal my loved one, I will rejoice and give you the glory. If you choose not to, I will still trust in you. May your good, pleasing, and perfect will be done in this situation and always. My prayer is in the powerful name of Jesus, your Son. Amen.

WHEN PRAYERS ARE UNANSWERED, EXAMINE YOURSELF

Lord, grant me pure thoughts—but not now!
—Augustine

When the Israelites were preparing to conquer the city of Jericho, God commanded them not to take any of the spoils of the battle. Everything was to be destroyed as a sacrifice to God. But on the day of battle, one man couldn't resist. Achan stole some gold, silver, and expensive clothing imported from Babylonia; and he hid them in his tent.

The next battle was against a little town—Ai. It was such a small city that Joshua only sent a few thousand men to conquer it. But the men of Ai routed them, and thirty-six Israelites were killed. The others came home defeated and embarrassed, wondering why God hadn't been with them as he was at Jericho.

When the defeated soldiers returned, Joshua tore his clothes, went into the tabernacle, fell to his knees before God, and begged for an explanation, praying, "Ah, Sovereign LORD, why did you ever bring this people across the Jordan to deliver us into the hands of the Amorites to destroy us?" (Joshua 7:7)

147

The Lord replied:

Stand up! What are you doing down on your face? Israel has sinned; they have violated my covenant, which I commanded them to keep. They have taken some of the devoted things; they have stolen, they have lied, they have put them with their own possessions. That is why the Israelites cannot stand against their enemies; they turn their backs and run because they have been made liable to destruction. I will not be with you anymore unless you destroy whatever among you is devoted to destruction. (Joshua 7:10–12)

God refused to hear the prayers of the Israelites until they were obedient, until they destroyed what he had commanded them to destroy. The next day God dramatically "called out" the one who had sinned—first by tribe, then by clan, then by family, and finally man by man, until Achan was chosen. Achan confessed what he had done and was executed for his crime. The things he had stolen were destroyed as God had commanded. Then the city of Ai was conquered with ease.

THE HINDRANCE OF SIN

The Israelites learned an important lesson: Sin in the camp weakens the army in the field. The same principle applies to the church and to the individual Christian. Not until sin is confronted, confessed, and purged will the power of God's Spirit flow through your life. If there is any sin you are unwilling to lay on the altar, your prayers will be negated. You don't have to be perfect for God to answer your prayers, but if you're living in deliberate defiance of God, your sin is a barrier between you and God. The Bible says:

> Surely the arm of the LORD is not too short to save, nor his ear too dull to hear. But your iniquities have separated you from your God; your sins have hidden his face from you, so that he will not hear. (Isaiah 59:1–2)

Besides Achan, there are many other examples in the Bible of sin's acting as a barricade between mankind and God. Adam and Eve had perfect fellowship with God until they sinned. Then they hid themselves from the Lord. They knew they didn't deserve to have his ear anymore. When God discovered their sin, they were removed from his presence and cast out of the Garden of Eden.

David knew that his unrepented sin had separated him from God. When he confessed, he wrote, "Create in me a pure heart, O God, and renew a steadfast spirit within me. Do not cast me from your presence or take your Holy Spirit from me" (Psalm 51:10–11). Another psalm explains, "If I had cherished sin in my heart, the Lord would not have listened; but God has surely listened and heard my voice in prayer" (Psalm 66:18–19).

King Saul wouldn't wait for Samuel to arrive to offer the sacrifice, even though Samuel had specifically commanded him to wait. It was not the king's place to act as priest. Saul disobeyed. He sacrificed and prayed anyway. "What can be wrong with praying?" Saul surely reasoned. Samuel told him: "Does the LORD delight in burnt offerings and sacrifices as much as in obeying the voice of the LORD? To obey is better than sacrifice, and to heed is better than the fat of rams" (1 Samuel 15:22). Samuel informed Saul that his throne would be taken away from him as a result of his disobedience. Yet Saul continued in rebellion against God, and the Bible says that the Lord left Saul and would no longer hear his prayers.

Whenever God doesn't answer one of our requests, the first thing we should do is examine our own hearts and lives. The problem may be with us. The Bible suggests that some of our hardship is the result of God's discipline:

> Endure hardship as discipline; God is treating you as sons. For what son is not disciplined by his father? If you are not disciplined (and everyone undergoes discipline), then you are illegitimate children and not true sons. Moreover, we have all had human fathers who disciplined us and we respected them for it. How much more should we submit to the Father of our spirits and live! Our fathers disciplined us for a little while as they thought best; but God disciplines us for our good, that we may share in his holiness. No discipline seems pleasant at the time, but painful. Later on, however, it produces a harvest of righteousness and peace for those who have been trained by it. (Hebrews 12:7–11)

Augustine prayed, "Lord, grant me pure thoughts—but not now!" We want answers to our prayers, but we're not willing to release our pride, our lust, our jealousy, or our greed. God doesn't want to be exploited. He's not some kind of sugar daddy waiting to give you anything your heart desires so you'll like him. He wants an intimate, authentic relationship with you—so he won't answer your prayer until you're willing to give up your sin and come back to a right relationship with him. We need to pray as David did: "Search me, O God, and know my heart: try me, and know my thoughts: And see if there be any wicked way in me, and lead me in the way everlasting" (Psalm 139:23–24 KJV).

Jesus doesn't want to be just a resident in your house. He wants to be the president. You might say to an overnight guest, "My house is your house. Make yourself at home." But you don't really mean it. You both know there are some places he shouldn't go. Maybe you've seen the advertisement in which a young woman is standing in the bathroom at her friend's house. "I sure love what you've done to the place!" she calls out, as she steals a peek inside the medicine cabinet. A sneer crosses her face when she notices a certain medication her friend has in the cabinet. When she reaches for the bottle to get a closer look, every shelf in the medicine cabinet comes crashing down! She faces terrible embarrassment because she has gone into an area of the house that is considered off-limits to a guest.

Jesus says to you, "Here I am! I stand at the door and knock. If anyone hears my voice and opens the door, I will come in and eat with him, and he with me" (Revelation 3:20). Jesus doesn't want to be an overnight guest. He wants to be Lord of your life. He wants to go into every closet, every cabinet, every basement corner, every attic box. Only when we open every phase of our lives to God and let him take control can we have compete fellowship with him and complete confidence that he is hearing our prayers.

The Bible specifically mentions several sins that, if not corrected, will hinder your prayers.

AN UNFORGIVING SPIRIT

Jesus said, "When you stand praying, if you hold anything against anyone, forgive him, so that your Father in heaven may forgive you your sins" (Mark 11:25).

Forgiving isn't easy. When someone wrongs you, it hurts. You instinctively want to get even. Your sense of justice has been violated. What the person did to you isn't right, and it certainly wouldn't be fair for you to just forgive him or her. But when you harbor ill feelings and bitterness toward someone, it short-circuits your communication with God. As long as you refuse to forgive, the power of prayer in your life will be diminished.

I mentioned earlier the parable Jesus told about the king who forgave his servant of a great debt only to discover that the servant left his presence, went out and found a man who owed him a very small debt, and demanded to be paid. The king was irate. Our King is not happy with us when he offers to forgive us of so great a debt, yet we refuse to forgive others who have wronged us.

I once met a man at Eddyville Prison who ministers to men on death row. After this man's daughter was murdered, his own bitterness was eating him alive. He couldn't find it in his heart to forgive the murderer. He decided to minister to men in prison as a way to release his anger. He knew that Scripture says, "If your enemy is hungry, give him food to eat;

if he is thirsty, give him water to drink" (Proverbs 25:21). The prisoners treat him like a hero, but he explained, "I'm not doing it for them—I'm doing it for me. It is for my release, that I might have a right relationship with God."

God wants us to really mean it when we pray, "Forgive our debts as we forgive those indebted to us." As long as we nurse bitterness or plot revenge, the power of prayer is limited in our lives.

MARITAL ESTRANGEMENT

The Bible says, "Husbands...be considerate as you live with your wives, and treat them with respect as the weaker partner and as heirs with you of the gracious gift of life, so that nothing will hinder your prayers" (1 Peter 3:7). Peter made it clear that if you're not getting along with your wife, God will not be as likely to hear your prayers. Marriage is supposed to be the highest, most spiritual of all human relationships. Jesus said that the Old Testament Law reluctantly included accommodations for divorce because of "the hardness of your hearts." But he explained that it was not meant to be so:

> At the beginning of creation God "made them male and female." "For this reason a man will leave his father and mother and be united to his wife, and the two will become one flesh." So they are no longer two, but one. Therefore what God has joined together, let man not separate. (Mark 10:6–9)

In Ephesians 5 Paul gave behavioral requirements for husbands and wives, saying that wives are to submit to their husbands as the church submits to Christ, and husbands are to love their wives as Christ loved the church and sacrificed himself for her. Paul quoted the same Old Testament passage Jesus had quoted ("For this reason a man will leave his father and mother and be united to his wife, and they will become one flesh" [Genesis 2:24]). Then Paul added, "This is a profound mystery—but I am talking about Christ and the church" (Ephesians 5:32). A Christian marriage relationship is to model to the world the love Christ has for his church.

If you're being a poor example, if you can't treat your mate with love and tenderness, if you can't listen to her or be patient with him, if you can't forgive the one closest to you, how can you expect God to treat you with those qualities?

When a husband and wife love each other and are joined in a genuine spiritual union, it's a wonderful testimony to the world, both partners are spiritually strengthened, and they can pray together knowing that God will hear their prayers. But when there is alienation between a husband and wife and bitterness is allowed to grow between them, it's nearly impossible for them to unite in prayer.

When I'm at odds with my wife, Judy, I have a hard time studying for my sermon. Preparing a sermon is a spiritual process that involves a lot of prayer and contemplation. It's hard to write a sermon about forgiveness or gratitude when you're harboring bitterness toward your wife. I have to stop working, go find Judy, and say, "Let's work this out."

It's impossible to have a perfect marriage, but when those inevitable disagreements come, work things out quickly.

"Do not let the sun go down while you are still angry" (Ephesians 4:26).

I remember a Christian leader who told about praying, "Lord, I haven't been treating my wife the way I should. I've been short-tempered, critical, and selfish. Please forgive me." This man said he could sense God's response: "Don't tell me—tell her!" Before you pray and ask God for his blessings, be sure you've made things right with your mate.

SELFISHNESS

The Bible says that sometimes our prayers aren't answered because we ask with improper motives:

> You want something but don't get it. You kill and covet, but you cannot have what you want. You quarrel and fight. You do not have, because you do not ask God. When you ask, you do not receive, because you ask with wrong motives, that you may spend what you get on your pleasures.
>
> You adulterous people, don't you know that friendship with the world is hatred toward God? Anyone who chooses to be a friend of the world becomes an enemy of God. (James 4:2–4)

We can make appropriate requests in our prayers but have selfish motivation. Someone might pray, "Lord, help me to reach my financial goals and get out of debt," but his motivation might be a desire for security, admiration from his peers, and personal pleasure instead of stewardship and generosity. Why should he expect God to satisfy those desires?

I might pray, "Lord, help me to preach well today." But if

my motive is ego-driven—I want people to admire me—then I shouldn't be surprised if God doesn't grant my request.

A young man who prays for a Christian wife may have self-centered motivation: He doesn't want to have to hold back his sex drive anymore. If he has no desire to minister to and provide for a well-deserving Christian woman, why should he expect God to satisfy his request?

Powerful prayer always has pure motives. For example, earlier I mentioned Elijah's prayer on Mount Carmel, when he called on God to bring fire from heaven. "Answer me, O LORD," Elijah prayed, "so these people will know that you, O LORD, are God, and that you are turning their hearts back again" (1 Kings 18:37). Elijah's motivation was not to gloat and be the hero but to glorify God. His prayer was answered in a dramatic way.

Contrast that with a prayer he uttered to God from a self-centered perspective just shortly after God brought down the fire. The wicked queen Jezebel was not happy with Elijah's victory, and she threatened to take his life. In fear, Elijah fled to the desert. After a day's journey, he fell exhausted under a broom tree and prayed that he might die. "I have had enough, LORD," he said. "Take my life; I am no better than my ancestors" (1 Kings 19:4). God wasn't finished with Elijah, so he didn't grant his request.

What a blessing that God didn't say yes to that selfish, egotistical, shortsighted prayer. When the time did come for Elijah to leave this world, he didn't die alone and depressed under a broom tree. Instead, in front of his friend and successor, Elisha, he was taken up to heaven in a fiery chariot. He went out in a blaze of glory! Elijah became one of only two men in history who never experienced death. He would have missed that glorious ending had God granted his self-centered request.

THE GOAL OF GROWTH

The reason God isn't answering your prayer may not have anything to do with sin. Maybe he just wants you to grow. As a parent might deny a child's request to stay home from school, God may deny your request because growth and development come through difficult tasks and circumstances. Discipline isn't always punishment for wrongdoing. An athlete disciplines himself not as punishment but so he will get stronger. And the stronger he becomes, the harder he must discipline himself to improve. Some of God's discipline may not be punishment at all, but rather his loving desire to see you grow stronger.

Have you ever had a prayer go unanswered and reasoned, "God must be displeased with me"? A lot of people think that if their prayers aren't answered, God must be angry with them. But when you consider that the prayers of Moses, Paul, and Jesus were not always answered affirmatively, you have to wonder if just the opposite might be true. C. S. Lewis, in a thought-provoking essay called "The Efficacy of Prayer," suggested as much:

> It would be [bad] to think of those who get what they pray for as a sort of court favorites, people who have

157

influence with the throne. The refused prayer of Christ in Gethsemane is answer enough to that.

And I dare not leave out the hard saying which I once heard from an experienced Christian: "I have seen many striking answers to prayer and more than one that I thought miraculous. But they usually come at the beginning: before conversion, or soon after it. As the Christian life proceeds, they tend to be rarer. The refusals, too, are not only more frequent; they become...more emphatic."

Does God then forsake just those who serve him best? Well, he who served him best of all said, near his tortured death, "Why hast thou forsaken me?" When God becomes man, that man, of all others is least comforted by God at his greatest need.

There is a mystery here which, if I had the power, I might not have the courage to explore. Meanwhile, little people like you and me, if our prayers are sometimes granted beyond all hope and probability, had better not draw hasty conclusions to our own advantage. If we were stronger, we might be less tenderly treated. If we were braver, we might be sent, with far less help, to defend far more desperate posts in the great battle.[1]

That's a challenging thought. Perhaps God treats more mature Christians with greater discipline to strengthen them.

Among all the letters I received from members of our congregation regarding answered prayer, one of the more thought-provoking letters was from Jennifer Heck, who was born with severe cerebral palsy and has had to battle her physical weaknesses every day of her life. Yet inside a crippled body is a brilliant mind and a gentle spirit. It takes her a much greater amount of time and effort to write a letter than it does most people, so I always appreciate any correspondence from Jennifer. And I wasn't surprised that her letter was among the deepest letters I have ever received. She wrote:

> We all experience suffering. Some people seem to experience more than their fair share, while others appear to have only minor occurrences of hardships. Yet heartache and trials are inevitable in this sin-stained and fallen world....God's sovereign ways, apparent periods of silence, and timing of events are beyond our capacity to comprehend. It helps to remember his ultimate goals for us are to know him more intimately; depend completely on him; and display his character, power, and glory....It is during times in the deserts and fiery furnaces of life that God refines the character of individuals more into the likeness of Jesus Christ.
>
> "Faith begins in the wilderness—when you are alone and afraid, when things don't make sense," shares Elisabeth Elliot...."In the wilderness of loneliness we are terribly vulnerable....But we may be missing the fact that it is here...here where we may learn to love him—here where it seems he is not at work, where his will seems obscure or frightening, where he is not doing what we expected him to do." Elliot concludes, "If faith does not go to work here it will not go to work at all."
>
> ...Therefore, in times of pain, hardship, loneliness, and uncertainty, the wisest thing we can do is ask one all-encompassing request, "God, please reveal yourself to me." This is a prayer he delights in answering.

THE PLACE OF FARTHER STILL

I like the phrase Bible teacher Beth Moore coined for intense prayer time with God. She calls it "the place of farther still."

The idea comes from the Gospels. Jesus was so burdened with the prospect of the cross that he went to the Garden of Gethsemane and left his disciples at the gate. He said, "You stay here and pray." He took Peter, James, and John into the inner garden and said, "You watch here and pray." Then Jesus went *farther still* into the garden to pray—to a place where his grief and pain were so intense that no one, not even those closest to him, could go with him. But he was not alone. The Father was faithful to meet him there, in "the place of farther still."

A father wrote to me about his prayers to God for his son who is HIV positive. The father is constantly burdened and concerned about his son's health and spiritual well-being. He shared that at times, the burden is more than he can bear. That's when he goes off by himself and pours out his heart to God, praying that God will be with him and give him the strength to go on. And God's grace is sufficient in "the place of farther still."

THE LIGHT OF GOD HIMSELF

When God refused to answer Paul's request to remove the thorn, God simply told him, "My grace is sufficient for you" (2 Corinthians 12:9). Warren Wiersbe wrote, "God didn't give any explanations, he just gave a promise: 'My grace is sufficient for you.' The response is in the perfect tense. It assumes continual application—the thorn will not be removed, but God's grace will be constant."[2]

Chapter Eight: EXAMINE YOURSELF

One of our church members, Kendrick McCandless, wrote about God's presence in her life after her mother died:

Shortly after I graduated from college, my mother died very suddenly; however, I cannot say it was totally unexpected. My mother had been an alcoholic as far back as I could remember and...was convinced that she was, in her words, "doomed to hell." Every discussion my younger sister and I initiated to dissuade her ended with my sister and me in tears and my mother calmly adamant that she had no hope.

My father found my mother one morning, lying unconscious on the floor, and called for emergency medical help. Unfortunately, they were not only unable to revive her, but they were also never able to tell us whether her death from a lethal mixture of alcohol and sleeping pills was accidental or self-induced. The days that followed her death were filled with the arrival of family members, plans for the funeral, and attempts to take care of my shocked and grieving father. But in time, the activities ended and the people went home.

One evening, I lay on my bed and let the true enormity of the previous week sink in, and I began to pray. This prayer was different from any prayer I had ever prayed before. It was a reaching out to God for answers at a time of deepest need. I knew I was telling him things he already knew, but I still needed to tell him everything—my fears, my confusion, my loss. I wanted to know where my mother was. I wanted to know that she was with him and that she was all right. I don't remember if I prayed out loud or silently. I do remember being completely distraught and crying uncontrollably. But when I came to the end of my words, I stopped and waited. And the most incredible sense of peace settled over me. This was a feeling I had never experienced before in my entire life, and I knew without a doubt that it came from God. For me this experience has been like the encounter Jacob had with the Lord at Bethel....

I'm sure people could say that my prayer was not answered. I still didn't know where my mother was. But I had a certainty that the Lord was in control, a certainty that has never wavered in the thirty-three years since I went to my heavenly Father with my questions and fears. I recently read something in a wonderful book by Dallas Willard, called *The Divine Conspiracy*. I think he says it best: "It is noteworthy that when Job finally stood before God he was completely satisfied and at rest, though not a single one of his questions about his sufferings had been answered. His questions were good questions. He did not sin in asking them. But in the light of God himself they were simply pointless. They just drop away and lose their interest."[3] I am so thankful that my prayer brought me into the "light of God himself."

GOD'S DESIRE FOR A RELATIONSHIP WITH YOU

More than almost anything else, God wants to be close to you. He wants to bring you into the light of himself. Though he doesn't cause most of the bad things that happen around you (he allows them as the result of a fallen world), one of the reasons he may choose not to intervene is that his relationship with you is more important to him than your personal comfort.

Several years ago, at a staff retreat, we were all asked to

list some of our personal prayer requests. I wrote, "Please pray for my wife. She's doing too much, and I think it's affecting her health. She needs to slow down."

Just a few weeks later, she suffered a stroke caused by a heart irregularity. Hundreds of people prayed for her recovery, and I thank God she did recover. But my initial prayer request for her protection wasn't answered. As a result, we went through some trying times—but she slowed down! I know she would never again want to go through the hospital stay, seizures, heart arrhythmia, exhaustion, medication, negative reaction to the medication, cardio shock treatment, or ablation surgery. But she'll tell you that she's a different person today because of what she experienced—she's closer to God and lives each day to the fullest. I told you she prays better than I do, and her experiences may be why. God didn't answer our initial prayers, but what he gave us was even better—a deeper walk with him and a greater appreciation for the things he has given us.

An anonymous poet wrote:

> *I asked God for strength that I might achieve;*
> *I was made weak that I might learn to humbly obey.*
> *I asked for health that I might do greater things;*
> *I was given infirmity that I might do better things.*
> *I asked for riches that I might be happy;*
> *I was given poverty that I might be wise.*
> *I asked for power that I might have the praise of men;*
> *I was given weakness that I might feel the need of God.*
> *I asked for all things that I might enjoy life;*

I was given life that I might enjoy all things.
I got nothing that I asked for, but everything I hoped for;
I am among all men most richly blessed.

WHEN THERE'S MORE TO IT

When God doesn't answer your prayer, the first thing to do is examine your own heart and life. Oswald Chambers, commenting on Matthew 7:9 ("Which of you, if his son asks for bread, will give him a stone?"), said:

> The illustration of prayer that our Lord used here is one of a good child who is asking for something good. We talk about prayer as if God hears us regardless of what our relationship is to Him....Never say that it is not God's will to give you what you ask. Don't faint and give up, but find out the reason you have not received; increase the intensity of your search and examine the evidence. Is your relationship right with your spouse, your children, and your fellow students? Are you a "good child" in those relationships? Do you have to say to the Lord, "I have been irritable and cross, but I still want spiritual blessings"? You cannot receive and will have to do without them until you have the attitude of a "good child."[4]

Are you living in a right relationship with God and others? Are your motives pure? If not, confess your sins and then come back to God with your needs.

If God still doesn't answer, remember this: Not all unanswered prayer is our fault. Jesus was perfect, yet his prayer in Gethsemane to bypass the cross was not answered affirmatively. Sometimes we have to admit we don't understand why God said no. What then?

Chapter Nine

WHEN PRAYERS ARE UNANSWERED, TRUST GOD

*Stand off in faith believing that what Jesus said is true, though
in the meantime you do not understand what God is doing.*
—Oswald Chambers, *My Utmost for His Highest*

I received a touching letter from a grandmother who asked,
"Dear Bob, why won't God answer? I have been praying for
fifteen years for a Christian man to come into the life of my
daughter and granddaughter—someone who can love them
and care for them as his very own." God hadn't answered
that prayer.

To make matters worse, the woman's daughter, a single
mom, discovered she has multiple sclerosis. Her ex-husband
has cut off child support, and there are several other challenging circumstances facing the family. The letter concluded, "So again I ask, where is God? I still pray and ask
God every day. But still no one is there."

Have you ever felt that way? You prayed for a mate, but
you're still single. You prayed for a baby, but you can't get
pregnant. You prayed your teenager would follow Christ,
but he drifted away from God. You prayed for financial

relief, but you're still in debt. You prayed for victory but suffered defeat. You prayed for a sick loved one, but death came. There will be times when God says no for reasons we don't understand.

That happened to Job. He knew, despite what his friends tried to tell him, that the problem was not his sin. God himself had commended Job as blameless and upright (Job 1:8). Something else was up. Job had examined himself. He knew God wasn't judging him for some hidden sin. It just didn't make sense. So why?

I can't tell you all the reasons why God doesn't answer our prayers affirmatively, but I can give you some things to think about the next time God says no.

TRUST GOD'S TIMING

Maybe God isn't saying no, but rather, wait. He may be insisting that you wait for his perfect timing. Perhaps God plans to answer your prayer, but in a greater way than you could have imagined.

Mary and Martha begged Jesus to come and heal their brother. It was a reasonable request. Lazarus was their provider. He was still young, a good man, and one of Jesus' best friends. But Jesus didn't answer their prayer for healing. Lazarus died. And Mary and Martha were upset. "Lord, if you had been here," they complained, "my brother would not have died" (John 11:21, 32).

Jesus wasn't just ignoring their request. He had something much greater in mind for them, and most importantly, something that would glorify God in a greater way. In just four days, they were going to witness one of the greatest miracles in history. God wasn't telling them no—he was just telling them to wait.

Sometimes, if we will wait on God's timing, we'll discover that God planned all along to answer our prayer in an even bigger and better way than we could have imagined. We want instant gratification, but God wants us to intensify our desires or refine our requests so he can give us something even better. You may have to wait for his perfect timing to receive the gift.

WAIT FOR A BETTER BALL GLOVE

Many years ago I promised to buy my son Rusty a baseball glove for his sixth birthday. We went into a drugstore where he spotted a shabby-looking glove on sale for five dollars. He said, "There's one, Daddy! Let's get that one!" I fully intended to buy him a glove, but I wanted to get one that was better and would last longer, so I said, "No, let's keep looking."

He began to cry right there in the store (which, Rusty would add, was very out of character!). "Please, Dad, let's get that one," he begged. I'm sure people were thinking, *Can you believe that mean dad won't even spend five bucks to buy his kid a baseball glove?* But I stood my ground and said, "No, I want to find another one that's better." He couldn't understand why I wouldn't buy him that glove. Later we went into a sporting goods store and found one that was a little more expensive but was a much better glove.

A few weeks later, I shared that story in a sermon to illustrate that sometimes God has something better in mind for us when he tells us no. Over a year later, a young man came up to me after church one day and said, "Awhile back, my fiancée jilted me on a Saturday night. I came to church the next day absolutely crushed, and you told that story about making your son wait for a better ball glove. That story really encouraged me, and I'm here today to ask you to perform my wedding. I've found a better 'ball glove'!"

SEE FARTHER AHEAD

I heard about an eight-year-old boy named Frank who for weeks had looked forward to going fishing with his father. But when the appointed Saturday arrived, it was raining heavily and looked as though it would continue all day long. His dad told a dejected Frank that they'd have to wait for another day to go fishing.

Frank moped around the house all morning, peering out the windows and grumbling a lot. His father tried to explain how badly the rain was needed—how God sent the rain to make the flowers grow and bring much-needed moisture to the farmers' crops. "But it seems like God would know that it would have been better to have rained yesterday than today," Frank complained. "It just isn't right," he kept saying.

About three o'clock in the afternoon, the rain stopped, and Frank's dad said there was still time for fishing. They quickly loaded their gear and headed for the lake. The fish were biting, and Frank and his dad had a great time. They returned with a string full of large fish. Dad cleaned them, and Mom fixed them for dinner.

When they sat down for supper, Frank's dad asked him to say the blessing. Frank concluded his prayer by saying, "And Lord, if I sounded grumpy earlier today, it was because I couldn't see far enough ahead."

When God isn't answering your prayer, try to look further ahead and speculate about how God may work it all out for good in his time.

Tom Wilson, a member of our church, wrote about one of their answers to prayer. He and his wife had been married for twelve years and had tried unsuccessfully to have children. He wrote:

> We were very involved in the children's program in our church in western New York and couldn't understand why God had given us this love for children but not blessed us with our own. We weren't angry, just confused and somewhat disappointed. We had been praying, but every time there seemed to be a glimmer of hope, a miscarriage wiped it out. The doctors said there was no medical explanation. We passed all the tests.
>
> Then one day we were sitting in church, a small congregation of about 250, when the pastor announced that a young mother in the community had been diagnosed with cancer and only had a few days to live. There was a three-year-old boy and an eight-month-old baby girl. The grandparents didn't feel capable of raising them, so they were asking for prayer and guidance.

Within a few weeks, the Wilsons adopted those two children. Today they are teenagers and active in our church.

Tom concluded, "Coincidence or answered prayer, you make the call. It all suddenly made sense why we had not been able to have children of our own over the years. In two weeks we had doubled the size of our family."

I recently visited a wonderful church in Sacramento, California. Their preacher, Rick Stedman, started the church ten years ago by sitting in front of a grocery store with a sign that said, "Would you like to get your kids off drugs?" He's a low-key, unassuming leader, but he has been faithfully teaching people God's Word, and today the church has more than five thousand members.

Just after Rick and his congregation had purchased land on which to relocate and construct a new church building, they discovered that the city's elite didn't want a church at that location. They wanted it to be used for developments that would reap large tax dividends for the city. So the town council called an emergency zoning ordinance revision meeting. The city's position was that there might be a toxic leak in the industrial zone, which might drift in the air over their property. The church argued was that right across the street from the property were houses and schools! If there was a toxic leak, they would be exposed too. The city said, "No, they are in a different zone," as if toxic leaks honor zoning laws! The real issue was that some of the businesses in the area were not in support of the church building in that location. It was a dirty deal, and the church rightly felt cheated.

During the hearing, Rick turned to the church's lawyer and asked, "Will I have a chance to speak?"

That wasn't the usual procedure, the attorney informed him. "But if you stand up and ask to say something, they may permit you to do so."

Rick prayed silently: *Lord, you said in your Word that if I am called in front of the authorities, you will give me the words to say. I don't know what to say, but I know I need to say something.*

The town council stubbornly took the low road and unanimously reversed a previous decision that had given the church permission to build on the property. It seemed like a dark hour for the church. But before the council was dismissed, Rick stood and said, "Mr. Mayor, may I say something?" He was granted permission to speak.

Rick later told me, "The Lord didn't give me anything to say! So I stalled. I said, 'Mr. Mayor, I want to thank you for giving me the opportunity to speak and for letting us plead our case before you today.'" Still nothing came from God. So Rick decided to stall further. He turned to the first council member and said, "Councilman Duncan, I want to thank you for listening today and for giving us a hearing." Still nothing came. So Rick turned to the city attorney and the city manager and repeated the message. When he came to the head planner, he could see a tear in her eye. Rick didn't know exactly what the Holy Spirit was doing, but he could tell God was at work. He thanked each councilperson individually. Still no wonderfully persuasive argument came from the Holy Spirit, so Rick concluded, "I guess that's all I want to say. We are a new church in town, and we are going

171

to work hard with you to make this a wonderful place to live. Thank you for the direction you've given us tonight, and we look forward to working with you in the future." He sat down.

"That's all you want to say?" the mayor asked, stunned.

"Yes sir, I guess so," Rick replied.

"We've had churches in here that have ripped us apart," the mayor mused. "They've threatened to vote us out of office for not doing what they want. And you come in here and thank us? We have never met a church like yours before. How can we help you find and build a church home?"

"I don't know," Rick said. "You just passed a law stating that we cannot build on the property we own."

After a pause, the mayor asked, "Would you accept a land trade if we offered it to you?"

Rick considered it a moment. "Well, if it was the same acreage and a good location, I guess we would."

The mayor looked toward the council and said authoritatively, "I want this church to have a good place to build their building. No one can develop or build on their present property until we find a suitable place to trade with them."

The church traded for an even better piece of property! It's located on a knoll in Sacramento. They're constructing a 3,500-seat auditorium with a cross on top that can be seen for two miles in any direction. The congregation is elated. What appeared to be unanswered prayer quickly proved to be the perfect hand of God at work.

SOME OF GOD'S GREATEST GIFTS ARE UNANSWERED PRAYERS

Sometimes we ask God for things that are not good at all. Several years ago entertainer Garth Brooks had a hit country song, "Thank God for Unanswered Prayers." In the song, he tells of running into his high school sweetheart at a football game. He remembers how much he loved her and how he prayed that God would give her to him as his wife. But now she doesn't look as good to him, and the conversation is awkward. He looks at her, then at his wife, and he says, "Sometimes I thank God for unanswered prayers!" He continues, "Just because he doesn't answer, doesn't mean he don't care. Some of God's greatest gifts are unanswered prayers!"[1]

Wayne Smith, the beloved former minister of Southland Christian Church in Lexington, Kentucky, underwent bypass surgery a few years ago. Prior to the surgery, during the heart catheterization, fifty-two people met in the chapel of St. Joseph's Hospital to pray for Wayne. Many of them prayed that the catheterization would reveal that his problem could be treated with medication, and surgery would not be necessary. Others prayed that the problem could be corrected with angioplasty, and the more invasive bypass surgery would not be needed. But God didn't answer those prayers. Bypass surgery was scheduled.

During the surgery, doctors discovered a hole in Wayne's pericardium, the sac that holds the heart. It was apparently a birth defect that had enlarged over the years, and his heart was sinking through the hole. There have only been 363 documented cases of this problem—all the others were discovered in autopsies.

The doctors said that if Wayne's situation had not been discovered in surgery, he would have lived just another six to twelve months. If they had attempted the less-invasive balloon surgery to open his arteries, it would have killed him. When it was first announced that Wayne would need surgery, I'm sure some people were disappointed that their prayers had not been answered. But thank God for unanswered prayer.

Years ago our church was badly in need of more space. We prayed that the neighbor would sell us his two-acre property so we could expand. We offered him four times what it was worth, and he refused to sell. We couldn't believe it, and we didn't understand why God hadn't answered our prayer. But his refusal to sell forced us down a different path. We eventually decided to purchase twenty-two acres and build a new facility. Our church exploded in growth in that new facility. We had been shortsighted, and we were asking for the wrong thing.

As the building was being built, the congregation fasted and prayed for our old church building to sell. We needed the money badly. But it never sold. We wondered why God didn't answer our prayers. But somehow we managed to pay the bills, and we kept the old building. After we moved out, for the next ten years we used that building as a youth center and second gymnasium. Our growth made that second building invaluable. I don't know what we would have done without it. When we decided to relocate a second time to our current facilities, we again found ourselves needing to sell that old building. This time it sold quickly (we praise God that we were able to sell *both* facilities), and that original building is being used by a vibrant congregation today. We didn't know it at the time, but God didn't answer our prayers because we were asking for the wrong thing at the wrong time. Thank God for unanswered prayer.

That's one reason we ought to pray, "Not my will but yours be done." We are wise to surrender in prayer to the authority and wisdom of an all-knowing God. The Bible says:

> The Spirit helps us in our weakness. We do not know what we ought to pray for, but the Spirit himself intercedes for us with groans that words cannot express. And he who searches our hearts knows the mind of the Spirit, because the Spirit intercedes for the saints in accordance with God's will.
>
> And we know that in all things God works for the good of those who love him, who have been called according to his purpose. (Romans 8:26–28)

TRY TO SEE IT FROM GOD'S PERSPECTIVE

Connie Wharton, a member of our church, wrote:

> My third child was born September 10, 1961, with a serious condition the doctors thought surgery would correct. The skin cells had not formed on her stomach, and the bowel had been pushed outside the

abdominal cavity. She was rushed to surgery in Children's Hospital without even the first hug from her mommy or daddy. We prayed for her the next thirty-six hours, asking God to give us a miracle—that he would allow her to live. He didn't. Her little body went for research so that doctors would be able to better treat this condition.

Seven years ago, a sister in Christ heard my testimony and shared with me that her daughter had been born with the sáme condition. Because research had allowed doctors to know how to better treat this condition in newborns, her daughter lived. I saw only the "seamy" side of the situation forty years ago and asked God why. But for the last seven years, I have been able to see it more from God's perspective.

Let's be honest. Sometimes when God doesn't answer, there's not a "something better" coming—at least not for us in this life. But try to see it from God's perspective. The reasons God does not honor your request may be complicated. It's a complex universe. God may be saying no to you so he can say yes to someone else. There may be a greater good out there—something that will somehow bring him greater glory.

IT'S NOT ABOUT YOU

I've learned that lesson myself in the last few years. Ever since our church relocated in 1998, it has been the best of times and the worst of times for me. The positive things that have happened in my ministry are obvious: incredible growth in the church, expanding influence, unimaginable joys in worship services, and the testimonies of changed lives. But I've had more stress, more problems, and more unanswered prayers in the last four years than during any other period in my life. I don't know whether it's satanic attack, God's pruning shears, or just the normal ebb and flow of life, but I've struggled. I haven't had the kind of pain that some others have, and I certainly haven't suffered the way Jesus did. Nevertheless, my struggles are my struggles, and they are serious to me.

When I'm tempted to get discouraged, I remember two truths that help my attitude.

First, *Suffering is inevitable, but misery is optional.* Jesus said, "In this world you will have trouble" (John 16:33). It's inevitable. But I can choose a positive attitude anyway.

Second, *It's not about me—it's about God.* God is not my servant who is supposed to respond to my every desire and make me comfortable. I'm his servant. I'm here to do his bidding. If he respects me enough to give me a tough assignment, I had better toughen up and follow through with the right spirit.

I once heard J. Vernon McGee say, "God designed and directs this universe, and we're here at his disposal. He owes us nothing. The fact that he communicates, sacrifices, dies, and provides is all so much more full of grace than we merit." We brazenly think we know better than God how to run the universe. If our prayers aren't answered the way we want them to be, we demand to know why. In our pride, we not only demand an explanation, we demand that God oversees the universe according to our limited perspective about right and wrong. Somebody said, "If you don't like the way God is running the universe, go start your own!" The Bible says:

> "My thoughts are not your thoughts, neither are your ways my ways," declares the LORD. "As the heavens are higher than the earth, so are my ways higher than your ways and my thoughts than your thoughts." (Isaiah 55:8–9)

WHY DID GOD TELL MOSES NO?

Consider the story we discussed earlier about Moses wanting to see the Promised Land. Why didn't God honor Moses' request? Try for a moment to see it from God's eternal perspective. Moses' punishment provided an unforgettable lesson to the entire nation that God requires obedience right up to the very end of life—even from the most dedicated leaders. Even though God forgave and saved Moses, disobedience has serious earthly consequences.

Besides, it was time for the mantle to be passed on to Joshua, a younger man. The people needed to learn how to get along without their miracle worker. They needed to see that God could work through someone else—someone like Joshua.

As soon as Moses was gone, God used Joshua to part the Jordan River during flood season so the people could cross on dry land, just as they had crossed the Red Sea under Moses' leadership forty years earlier. The people realized that the power of God was now with Moses' successor, and they confidently followed Joshua. That transition would not have taken place smoothly if Moses had still been around.

So God said to Moses, "Commission Joshua, and encourage and strengthen him, for he will lead this people across and will cause them to inherit the land that you will see" (Deuteronomy 3:28).

Though he didn't permit Moses to enter Canaan, God did lead him to a high mountain on a clear day where Moses was given a spectacular view of the region. God knew that entering the Promised Land would not be all glamour and glory. There would be brutal wars, a few defeats, and many hardships and disappointments. It was too much for an old man. It was time for Moses to check out of this difficult world and receive his reward. God had a better Promised Land in mind for him. When Moses pleaded, "Let me just walk out onto the playing field where the victory is going to be realized," God said, "No, Moses. Come on up here in the press box where it's dry and warm, and let's watch this all unfold together—just you and me."

So Moses climbed the mountain, enjoyed the view for a few moments, and died. God buried Moses' body and gathered his soul to himself. The day after Moses' death, if you had asked him if he would have preferred to cross the Jordan with the Israelites or climb Mount Nebo and be with God, I'm sure it wouldn't have been a close call. Moses would quickly reply, "I'm glad God didn't answer my prayer. To depart and be with the Lord is far better."

WHY DID GOD TELL PAUL NO?

Consider, also, the story we discussed earlier of Paul's thorn in the flesh. Why did God refuse to remove Paul's thorn? It's difficult to understand from a human perspective, but try to see it from God's eternal perspective.

Paul said, "To keep me from becoming conceited because of these surpassingly great revelations, there was given me a thorn in my flesh" (2 Corinthians 12:7). Paul battled pride all his life. That's understandable—he was smarter, better educated, more experienced, and more gifted than any of the other apostles. He also had been privileged to have special revelations and visions from God. He'd even been given a special tour of heaven where he saw "inexpressible things" (2 Corinthians 12:1–6). Everywhere he went, the Christians probably doted on him and told him how wonderful he was and how privileged they felt to meet him.

When you've been in the ministry a long time, like I have (nearly forty years), people praise you a lot—to the point that you can begin to believe you really are someone special. I had the biggest ego boost of my ministry recently. I got on a plane and sat down by a stranger. As I buckled my seat belt, I noticed he was reading one of my books, *When God Builds a Church*. What an honor! At first I didn't know whether to say anything or not. I didn't have to. He looked over at me with a strange expression, and then turned to the flyleaf to get a second look at my picture. He stuck the book in front of me and said, "Would you sign this?" During the flight, he asked me some questions about the book and told me it was an honor to meet me. When I got off the plane an hour later, my head would barely fit through the door. I felt like I was really somebody important.

God knew the attention and accolades could cause Paul to grow conceited, so to keep him humble, he denied Paul's request for physical healing. He said, "My grace is sufficient for you." In essence, God was saying, "I've saved your soul, and that's enough. I'll give you the strength to deal with these other issues. I want you to keep trusting in me. You think you'll be more effective without this physical handicap, but actually, you're more effective because of it." Paul, determined to trust in Christ, responded:

> Therefore I will boast all the more gladly about my weaknesses, so that Christ's power may rest on me. That is why, for Christ's sake, I delight in weaknesses, in insults, in hardships, in persecutions, in difficulties. For when I am weak, then I am strong. (2 Corinthians 12:9–10)

David Ring was a guest speaker at our church several years ago. David has cerebral palsy and a severe speech impediment, but he travels the country, preaching the gospel to thousands of people. In his weakness, he is strong. His humble presentation and his joy in spite of a severe disability allow him to break down barriers and soften hearts.

I've heard David talk about how difficult his childhood was. His classmates were merciless and constantly made fun of him. He was very attached to his mother, who loved him. She was the only one who gave him hope. When his mother got sick, he prayed that she'd get well. "God, please don't take my momma—she's all I've got," he prayed. But she didn't get well.

Despite unanswered prayers and daily physical struggles, David Ring has found hope in Christ. He's not bitter. He has used his weakness to glorify God. When he preaches through his speech impediment he will say, "Dey said I would nebbew wide a bike, but I did. Dey said I would nebbew get mawied, but I did. I got five chilwen to pwove it! Dey said I would nebbew pweach. But last yeaw, I pweached 253 times. Now, I hab cewebwal pawsy. What's yo' pwoblem?"

People love David Ring. His thorn in the flesh endears him to his audience. If he had no speech impediment, he would be a good preacher, but not nearly as powerful as he is with the impediment. Somehow, in his weakness, God becomes strong. His mother probably prayed for a healthy child. But God had something in mind that would bring glory to himself in a greater way, and that involved allowing David to suffer with cerebral palsy.

David says, "I'm impewfect. God has me in de oven wight now. I'm not finished. I don't like de heat, but one day he's gonna take me outa de oven and say, 'Hmmm...Well done, good and faithfuw sewvant!'"

CONSIDER THE IMPACT FOR CHRIST

As David Ring has exemplified, God may intend to glorify himself through your weakness or trial. Anne Wegert's mother, Sally Wortham, passed away fifteen years ago.

Anne wrote of the positive impact her mother's death has had on scores of people:

> To this day, though I have prayed about and for many things, there is nothing that I have prayed harder for than I did when mom was so sick and weak with cancer...and she died. If the picture were that simple, I suppose my family would have to believe we had been either ignored or let down by God. I am eternally grateful that the picture is so much more beautifully complex than that. From the day she was diagnosed, Momma faithfully quoted Romans and promised, "something good will come of this." I watched her responsibly fight her illness, and gracefully die with peaceful dignity. And you know what? So much "good" has come from this.
>
> Though her illness was, for the most part, long on heartache and short on victory, the number of people who were drawn closer to Christ through it is amazing. My mom, a public schoolteacher, took advantage of her role and influence in the classroom to let her students know that though she longed for a medical cure, her ultimate hope was in Jesus Christ. Many of her former students have told me of her outspoken faith. Through these last fifteen years, I have been surprised to have been called or written notes of encouragement by so many who fondly remember Momma....
>
> I envisioned a huge hole in our futures upon her passing—what about our weddings? What about grandchildren? You know what? When I got engaged, I had scads of "mothers" from this wonderful church family popping up in every direction, and not a detail nor emotional need was left unmet. And those grandchildren?

My dad has since married a godly, wonderful woman who embraces my children as her own and calls me one of her daughters.

One of our staff members, Mike Smith, says that his life's story is also one of unanswered prayer that God used for a greater glory. He was distraught when, in 1984, his fifteen-month-old son became ill and died. But the experience, along with the prayers of Mike's wife, Cynthia, led Mike to commit his life to Christ.

Mike and Cynthia decided they wanted to have another child, but doctors told them it was impossible because of a surgery Mike had undergone a few years earlier. But prayer works! They were able to conceive again, and their son Adam is now a healthy, six-foot-four-inch teenage athlete and a great young man. As a result of an experience with unanswered prayer, Mike will spend eternity in heaven—with both his sons.

Perhaps the most dramatic example of unanswered prayers having an impact for Christ can be seen in the story of Jim Elliot and the other missionaries who were martyred fifty years ago by the Auca Indians they were trying to reach. The prayers of their family members for their safety went unanswered. The prayers of the missionaries themselves for the salvation of the tribe seemed also to go unanswered. But God had a greater glory in mind. Because of their dramatic sacrifice, thousands of young people have been inspired to enter the mission field. And many of those same Auca Indians were eventually led to Christ by relatives of the slain missionaries. These former murderers have gone on to lead people in neighboring tribes to Jesus Christ!

HOLD ON TO YOUR FAITH

When God doesn't answer your prayer, keep trusting in his goodness and his providence. There will be times when you can't see any possible good coming from your situation. Sometimes there's nothing you can do except hold on to your faith. With Job, you can say, "Though he slay me, yet will I hope in him" (Job 13:15).

REMEMBER, GOD IS STILL WITH YOU

Some Native American tribes had a peculiar rite of passage when a boy reached the age of thirteen. The boy was blind-folded, led out into the woods, and left to spend the night alone. It was a test of his courage and manhood to see if he could sit and listen to the sounds of the night without crying out for help or attempting to return to the safety of his mother's tepee. When the morning light finally came, he would discover that his father was sitting just a few feet away from him. Though he did not know it, his father had been there all along, in the dark, protecting him and watching over him.

In 1949 eleven communist leaders were on trial in New York for conspiracy to overthrow the government by violence. The highly publicized trial, over which Judge Medina presided, went on for eight months. J. Wallace Hamilton, in *Where Now Is Thy God?* recalled his impressions of that historic event: "The behavior of the Communists was abominable. They were insolent, arrogant, did everything in their power to secure a mistrial."

Hamilton kept a clipping out of the *St. Petersburg Independent*, where Judge Medina spoke of his experiences. The article says that around the seventh month of the trial, Medina felt he was going to pieces—his nerves were frayed by the constant bickering and the telephone calls threatening his life and the lives of his loved ones. He felt he was on the verge of collapse. Medina told the press about one spiritual moment that allowed him to make it through:

> One day I had to leave the courtroom. My head suddenly began to swim. I recessed the court and walked quickly to the little room at the back and lay down. I felt panicky, and I'll be frank about it, I was certain that I could never go back. I had stood as much as a human being could endure. I knew I would have to quit. But suddenly, there in the little room, I found myself like a frightened child calling to his father in the dark. I asked God to help me, just to take charge, that his will might be done. I cannot report anything mysterious or supernatural, there was no vision or visitation, all I know is that as I lay on the couch, some new kind of strength flowed into me. I was in that little room for only fifteen minutes, but that brief communion with my God saved not only the trial but my sanity as well. I opened the door and walked again to the bench with a firm realization that I could take whatever was ahead.[2]

Remember Jeremiah's complaint? "You have covered yourself with a cloud," he lamented to God. But just a few verses later, Jeremiah admitted that when he called out, God came. "I called on your name, O LORD, from the depths of the pit. You heard my plea: 'Do not close your ears to my cry for relief.' You came near when I called you, and you said, 'Do not fear'" (Lamentations 3:55–57).

You may never understand why God doesn't answer all of your prayers. But rest assured, in your darkest hour, he will be there with you to comfort you and see you through. The psalmist wrote, "In my alarm I said, 'I am cut off from your sight!' Yet you heard my cry for mercy when I called to you for help" (Psalm 31:22).

TRUST GOD IN THE MIDST OF THE STORM

Anne Wegert's brother, Tom Wortham, has been through his share of life's trials. In the fall of 2001 Tom and his wife, Tammy, discovered that their two-year-old son, Taylor, had a brain tumor. A risky thirteen-hour emergency neurosurgery was required to remove the tumor and give Taylor any hope of living. Tom and Tammy's family members and dozens of lifelong friends and members of their Bible Fellowship class camped out at the hospital to pray for Taylor and to support the family.

The surgery was somewhat successful, and we all thanked God for answered prayer. But a year of chemotherapy followed to attempt to remove the rest of the tumor. Friends and family held a yearlong prayer chain for the Worthams as they endured the side effects, blood count irregularities, financial burdens, and quarantines from other children. I can't think of anything that would test your faith more than a prolonged, severe illness in one of your small children.

Taylor is now finished with his chemotherapy, and God has answered a lot of prayers, but the long-term prognosis is still unknown. In spite of uncertainties about Taylor's future, Tom and Tammy continue to hold out hope that God will answer their prayers, and remarkably, they continue to trust in the goodness of God. Tammy wrote about how she has attempted to overcome the temptation to become bitter:

> I picture us in a boat in the middle of a storm. Though you're surrounded by the storm, you know that God is in the front of the boat. And you know He never abandons the ship. We know God has been in this boat with us from the beginning. He's not jumping out now. And when I cuddle Taylor in my lap, I picture Jesus holding all of us. We don't like what we've been through this year, and there have been times when we just sit in our Father's lap and cry, but we don't lose faith in our Father.

With all they have been through, if Tom and Tammy Wortham can continue to trust God's goodness when he denies their request for healing, surely I, too, can trust him when I don't get my way.

ONLY GOD IS GOD

In an earlier chapter, I told you about a young lady named Karen Brown. After her first husband died of lung cancer that metastasized to the brain, Karen's in-laws prayed that she would find a new husband, and God dramatically answered their prayer. When she heard that I had used her letter in a sermon and that I had also told the story of Brett DeYoung's healing from a similar brain cancer, it brought up some very deep emotions in her. She told her second husband, Ken Brown, that even though she knew God had answered so many of her prayers, and she knew her first husband, Russ, was in heaven, she wondered at times why her prayers for Russ weren't answered.

"Why did God listen to all those prayers for Brett DeYoung and he was healed," she asked, "when just as many people prayed for Russ, and his brain tumor was malignant and fatal?"

Ken wrote:

I had no answers or words of comfort. Why would God so quickly answer the prayer from [Karen's former in-laws] for a new husband for their widowed daughter-in-law and fatherless grandson when just fifteen months earlier he had seemingly ignored the pleas from that same desperate mother and father for healing of their own son's life? Why answer one prayer and not the other? Why was it necessary that in order for my life to be so unbelievably blessed with a loving wife and fantastic children, that someone else had to die?

As long as I am on this earth, I guess I will never know. First Corinthians 13:12 says, "Now we see but a poor reflection as in a mirror; then we shall see face to face. Now I know in part; then I shall know fully, even as I am fully known." I know there will come a day in heaven [when]...suddenly God is going to reveal his ultimate plan so clearly that [we] will finally know in full.

Another of our church members, Tony O'Daniel, wrote about his own experiences and questions of faith:

In 1974 our son was born two months premature and was rushed to Norton Children's Hospital. The attending doctors told us that...he would probably not survive the

189

hour and certainly not the night. They told us that if he survived, he could be mildly to severely brain damaged and possibly have a limp due to a large hematoma on his foot that developed in their attempts to feed him through the IVs. My wife, Necie, and I came from large Christian families and had a large Christian support base in extended family and friends. The prayers offered for our son were innumerable. Thirty-six days later, he was removed from his respirator, and I held my son for the first time. His survival led one of his attending physicians to refer to him as the miracle baby whose recovery transcended...medical technology.

But five years after their son was born, Necie, a vibrant young thirty-two-year-old woman in excellent health, was diagnosed with cancer. Once again, the flood of prayers from family and friends for another miracle began. But God didn't answer those prayers. She died two years later.

Tony wrote, "Why? The answer is never clear amidst the grief. Why was our one miracle granted, the answer to our prayers acknowledged in circumstances that defy medical reasoning, and yet this wonderful, wholesome woman was taken?" The unyielding faith of his wife's mother, who had endured trial after trial in her life, and the faith of other believers helped Tony find the answer. "God's way is not man's way," he concluded, "and sometimes we have to have the strength to believe yet not understand."

Chapter Ten

WHEN PRAYERS ARE UNANSWERED, FOCUS ON ETERNITY

*God answers every prayer, for either he gives what we
pray for, or something far better.*

—Sören Kierkegaard

My son Phil took his wife, Lisa, to the hospital when they
suspected she was having another miscarriage. After some
tests, Lisa was called into the doctor's office to meet with Dr.
Boerner, who is a member of our church. He said, "We don't
have good news. The baby is gone. This is God's will sometimes, even though we don't understand it. We'd like to
have prayer with you, if that's OK."

They all joined hands and prayed. Through her tears,
Lisa later told me, "It was so comforting to have them pray
for me and to be reminded that I still have hope. God is still
in control. There will be a better day."

When your prayers aren't answered and you can't understand God's will, remember the Bible's promise: "Weeping
may remain for a night, but rejoicing comes in the morning"
(Psalm 30:5).

Though I disagree with much of what Sören Kierkegaard
wrote, I like what he said about prayer: "God possesses all

good gifts, and his bounty is greater than human under-standing can grasp. This is our comfort, because God answers every prayer; for either he gives what we pray for, or some-thing far better."

Elisabeth Elliot, widow of martyred missionary Jim Elliot, wrote:

> Heaven is not here, it's there. If we were given all we wanted here, our hearts would settle for this world rather than the next. God is forever luring us up and away from this one, wooing us to himself and his still invisible king-dom, where we will certainly find what we so keenly long for.[1]

In our final chapter, let's take some time to focus on the "something far better" to which we look forward.

Historically, when life has been difficult, Christians have focused on heaven. The first-century Christians who lived under persecution longed for the day when Christ would return. "Come quickly, Lord Jesus," they prayed. In the early history of the United States, Christian slaves focused on heaven. "This world is not my home, I'm just passing through," they would sing. Or, "I'm just a poor, way-faring stranger, traveling through this world of woe." That hope of heaven empowered them to endure difficult times.

Sometimes we don't focus much on heaven because we have it so good down here on earth. We're not living in per-secution or poverty, and our roots can go down pretty deep in this affluent, comfortable world. We might even picture heaven as a boring place, where people sit on a cloud and strum harps all day. But when your prayers go unanswered and this world becomes difficult, heaven begins to look a lot more attractive. And when you understand what heaven is *really* all about, you can't wait to get there.

The Bible instructs us to set our minds on things above, to store up treasure in heaven, to fix our eyes on things that are unseen. "Thy kingdom come. Thy will be done," Jesus instructed us to pray (Matthew 6:10 KJV). The very first part of Jesus' model prayer was focused on the future—on the kingdom to come, the point in time when Jesus will return and make all things right. In order to have the proper perspective toward things on earth, whether good or bad, Jesus knew that we must regularly anticipate the kingdom of heaven.

I'd like to take some time at the close of this book to help you imagine what heaven is going to be like. Then, the next time your prayers are unanswered and life seems difficult, you can remember what Paul said to the Romans: "I consider that our present sufferings are not worth comparing with the glory that will be revealed in us" (Romans 8:18).

WHY WE SHOULD FOCUS ON HEAVEN

There are at least three reasons we should try to take our focus off this world and set our minds on things above.

IT REDUCES OUR ATTRACTION TO THE WORLD

The Bible says:

> Do not love the world or anything in the world. If anyone loves the world, the love of the Father is not in him.

For everything in the world—the cravings of sinful man, the lust of his eyes and the boasting of what he has and does—comes not from the Father but from the world. The world and its desires pass away, but the man who does the will of God lives forever. (1 John 2:15–17)

When our primary focus is heaven, we'll recognize that this world is temporary, and we won't get so enamored of it. We won't be as bothered when our prayers go unanswered, because we'll recognize that life on this earth is short compared with eternity in heaven. We won't put our hope in the things of this world, because we'll understand that this world and everything in it is destined for destruction (see 2 Peter 3:10).

A man in our congregation showed me an advertisement for New York City that he found in a gourmet magazine published in the 1990s. In the picture, you can see the twin towers and the lights that read, "I Love NY." You can also see a cross that stands above one of the World Trade Center towers. I don't know how or why that cross was there, but I found it symbolic—that above the world's tallest building was the cross of Christ. He is above all.

Then I noticed that the advertisement said, "Stop by. The light's always on. The fun and excitement of New York City just never stops." But on September 11, 2001, it did stop.

Even the world's most impressive buildings will someday pass away. We had better have our hope in something beyond this world. If our hope is primarily in heaven, we won't be terrified even when our world collapses and our prayers aren't answered as we'd like. We won't be jealous of those who have more of this world's goods. We won't be as tempted by the temporary pleasures of this world. And we won't be so easily discouraged by suffering and pain, because we'll understand that it's just a passing part of our experience in this world.

IT GIVES US A PERMANENT HOPE FOR THE FUTURE

Focusing on heaven also gives us a permanent hope. No matter what happens in this life—no matter how many prayers go unanswered—we know there will come a day when all things will be made right. First Peter 1:3–9 says:

> Praise be to the God and Father of our Lord Jesus Christ! In his great mercy he has given us new birth into a living hope through the resurrection of Jesus Christ from the dead, and into an inheritance that can never perish, spoil or fade—kept in heaven for you, who through faith are shielded by God's power until the coming of the salvation that is ready to be revealed in the last time. In this you greatly rejoice, though now for a little while you may have had to suffer grief in all kinds of trials. These have come so that your faith—of greater worth than gold, which perishes even though refined by fire—may be proved genuine and may result in praise, glory and honor when Jesus Christ is revealed. Though you have not seen him, you love him; and even though you do not see him now, you believe in him and are filled with an inexpressible and glorious joy, for you are receiving the goal of your faith, the salvation of your souls.

You may be suffering from all kinds of trials, your prayers may have gone unanswered, and you may wonder how God could ever provide a way out. Maybe you were scarred so deeply in your childhood that you know you'll never completely get over it in this life. Maybe you're so far in debt that you'll probably be battling uphill the rest of your life. Maybe you went through a bitter divorce—or two—and you have children from each marriage who are suffering because of it. Maybe a loved one died, and you know you'll never see him or her again on this earth. If your primary focus is on this present world, you'll become increasingly discouraged and depressed. But if your citizenship is in heaven, you have a hope that can never spoil or fade. Second Corinthians 4:16–18 says:

> Therefore we do not lose heart. Though outwardly we are wasting away, yet inwardly we are being renewed day by day. For our light and momentary troubles are achieving for us an eternal glory that far outweighs them all. So we fix our eyes not on what is seen, but on what is unseen. For what is seen is temporary, but what is unseen is eternal.

God promises to give you a fresh start. One day he's going to make all things new. He promised the Israelites through the prophet Joel, "I will repay you for the years the locusts have eaten" (Joel 2:25). What a great image that is. The locusts of this world may have eaten away many years of your life. God promises he will restore those years—many times over—in a perfect eternity. The greatest enemy of all—death—will be defeated, and we will live forever with God.

I heard about three old men who were asked what they would like people at their funeral to say about them while viewing their bodies lying in their caskets.

The first said, "I'd like for people to say, 'He was a generous man.'"

The second man said, "I hope people will say, 'He was a good family man.'"

The third man said, "I want them to say, 'Look, he's moving!'"

Isn't that what we all want? We hope that there is life beyond the grave. The Bible promises: "If the Spirit of him who raised Jesus from the dead is living in you, he who raised Christ from the dead will also give life to your mortal bodies through his Spirit, who lives in you" (Romans 8:11).

There's tremendous energy in hope. You can overcome a lot of unanswered prayers if your ultimate hope lies in the next life. A philosopher once said, wisely, "If a man has a *why* for living, he can endure any *how.*" If your reason for living is to serve God and to prepare for a life in eternity with him, with God's help, you can make it through anything.

The Bible says that Moses "chose to be mistreated along with the people of God rather than to enjoy the pleasures of sin for a short time. He regarded disgrace for the sake of Christ as of greater value than the treasures of Egypt, because he was looking ahead to his reward" (Hebrews 11:25–26). As we discussed earlier, Moses had nothing to gain in this world by obeying God's call to lead the people out of Egypt. It was a difficult forty years for him, and in the end, he didn't even get to enter the Promised Land. But Moses' hope for an eternal reward was powerful enough to motivate him to endure the hardships and lead the people as God wanted. When we have hope of life beyond death, it empowers us to live with vitality and optimism, even when our prayers seem to go unanswered.

IT SATISFIES OUR LONGING FOR SOMETHING MORE

Do you ever look at a fish in a bowl and feel sorry for the fish? He has plenty to eat and some water to swim in, but he's not fully contented in that bowl, because he's not in his natural environment. He was created for the freedom and challenge of a larger body of water. Since he's confined to a small bowl, he keeps nudging into the sides of the tank. That fish has never been in a lake, but instinctively he knows he doesn't belong where he is. He was created for something more, and he seems to long for it in spite of the fact that he's never seen it.

You are a child of God, living in a restricted globe—somewhat like the fish. You have food, air, and companions here, and sometimes you have all you need. But instinctively you know that you were created for something more—something beyond what you're experiencing here.

Solomon said that God has set eternity in our hearts (Ecclesiastes 3:11). David wrote: "As the deer pants for streams of water, so my soul pants for you, O God" (Psalm 42:1). Even comedian Jim Carey spoke seriously of "the giant black hole that is my need," speaking of his need for affirmation that he couldn't seem to fill. There is a restlessness in every heart that longs for more. We try more pleasure, more possessions, more power—even more religion. But we're like the fish that keeps bumping up against the glass barrier. We're not satisfied. The apostle Paul said, "We groan, longing to be clothed with our heavenly dwelling" (2 Corinthians 5:2).

In *Mere Christianity* C. S. Lewis wrote:

Creatures are not born with desires unless satisfaction for those desires exists. A baby feels hunger: well, there is such a thing as food. A duckling wants to swim: well, there is such a thing as water. Men feel sexual desire: well, there is such a thing as sex. If I find in myself a desire which no experience in this world can satisfy, the most probable explanation is that I was made for another world. If none of my earthly pleasures satisfy it, that does not prove that the universe is a fraud. Probably earthly pleasures were never meant to satisfy it, but only to arouse it, to suggest the real thing.[2]

Jim Carey may not know it, but only God can fill the giant black hole. When we focus on the room we've been promised in God's house, where we'll be living in the presence and under the care of the Father forever, that inner longing for something more begins to be satisfied.

Have you ever gone to church or to a special revival meeting feeling kind of empty or depressed, but then something happened there to quicken your spirit? Maybe it was a song that inspired you, an Easter pageant that made you cry, or a sermon that whetted your appetite. In those moments, you can almost feel your soul being fed. You move forward in your seat, shut out everything around you, and sense that something special is happening. When you hear about God's promises, when you are fed God's Word, when you praise God's name with God's people, something about it rings true in your spirit. You leave with a totally different feeling and a completely different attitude than you had when you started.

That's all just a foretaste—a sample—of how your spirit will be fed every day in heaven. Peter wrote, "Though you have not seen him, you love him; and even though you do not see him now, you believe in him and are filled with an inexpressible and glorious joy, for you are receiving the goal of your faith, the salvation of your souls" (1 Peter 1:8–9). When we focus on heaven, our souls get fed.

HOW WE CAN FOCUS ON HEAVEN

Paul said, "Since, then, you have been raised with Christ, set your hearts on things above, where Christ is seated at the right hand of God" (Colossians 3:1). If you were planning a trip to Hawaii, you'd be really excited about it—even if you'd never been there—because you have a good idea of what it's going to be like. You've seen videos of flowers and waterfalls. You've read about the golf courses, the beaches, and the fish. You've talked to people who have visited Hawaii and come back to tell of its beauty. You haven't been there, but you can look forward to it because you can imagine it. You might even go so far as to plan your itinerary: "We're going to swim, hike, sightsee, fish, parasail, snorkel..."

At first, it may be hard to get as excited about a trip to heaven because it's a little harder to imagine what heaven will be like. We don't have videos or pictures. The Bible doesn't give us a lot of details. Even those who have been there and returned have a hard time describing it. The apostle Paul was allowed to see what he called "the third heaven."[3] He said he saw things he wasn't permitted to tell (2 Corinthians 12:4). But he did say that if he had his choice, he'd rather depart and be with the Lord because that is "better by far" (Philippians 1:23).

Maybe God doesn't give us more information about heaven because, if we knew more about it, we'd be so heavenly minded, we would be no earthly good! Or maybe it's just indescribable, and we aren't capable of grasping it. Maybe describing heaven in our limited vocabulary is like trying to describe Hawaii to a three-year-old. The Bible says, "No eye has seen, no ear has heard, no mind has conceived what God has prepared for those who love him" (1 Corinthians 2:9).

But God has given us an imagination, and he expects us to use it for good. So let's imagine what heaven will be like. As I list these things the Bible tells us will be in heaven, try to imagine what your first day in heaven will be like.

GOD THE CREATOR WILL BE THERE

John described heaven at the end of Revelation: "I heard a loud voice from the throne saying, 'Now the dwelling of God is with men, and he will live with them. They will be his people, and God himself will be with them and be their God'" (Revelation 21:3).

Think of the privilege of living where God lives and seeing him personally. The Bible says that "now we see through a glass darkly; but then face to face" (1 Corinthians 13:12 KJV). Think about it: You're going to have a personal encounter with Almighty God, the Creator of the universe, the Savior of your soul! I've heard people say, "The first thing I'm going to do when I see the Lord is run up to him and give him a great big hug!" Well, that might be the second thing you do. But the first thing you'll do when you come into the presence of perfect holiness is fall on your knees in worship.

You're going to meet the God to whom you've been praying all these years, and about whom you've been singing in all those worship services. What a spectacular moment that will be! We used to sing: Just to look upon his face, the one who saved me by his grace, what a glorious day that will be!

RELIEF AND HEALING WILL BE THERE

John wrote in the Book of Revelation, "He will wipe every tear from their eyes. There will be no more death or mourning or crying or pain, for the old order of things has passed away" (Revelation 21:4).

Think about some of the things that *won't* be in heaven. *We won't cry out in pain or grief anymore.* There will be relief from the throbbing wounds of this world. *We won't be dragged down by the flesh anymore.* We'll be free from the temptations of these mortal bodies and carnal minds. *We won't be limited by aging or disabilities anymore.* I think about some of the people in our congregation who have disabilities, and what heaven will be like for them: Jennifer Heck will be able to speak clearly and walk without a limp. Turley Richards will see. Kathy Kiper will get out of her wheelchair and walk. Vernon Gordon will be able to hear. Dale Mowery will have hair! I will be six-feet-three-inches tall and have broad shoulders. The old order of things will have passed away. Paul wrote:

> I declare to you, brothers, that flesh and blood cannot inherit the kingdom of God, nor does the perishable inherit the imperishable. Listen, I tell you a mystery: We will not all sleep, but we will all be changed—in a flash, in the twinkling of an eye, at the last trumpet. For the trumpet will sound, the dead will be raised imperishable, and we will be changed. For the perishable must clothe itself with the imperishable, and the mortal with immortality. When the perishable has been clothed with the imperishable, and the mortal with immortality, then the saying that is written will come true: "Death has been swallowed up in victory." (1 Corinthians 15:50–54)

WORSHIP AND INSPIRATION WILL BE THERE

The Bible indicates that heaven will be a place where we worship Christ, where we will "fall down before him who sits on the throne, and worship him who lives for ever and ever" (Revelation 4:10). If you're a healthy Christian, you look forward to special times of worship. You get excited about attending a special event where Michael W. Smith is leading worship or Max Lucado is preaching or your favorite group is singing. Just think of the inspirational worship services we'll have in heaven! Every week—every day—will be spectacular. Imagine the conversations each morning: "The angels are going to sing today!" "I heard Gabriel will be playing the trumpet!" "Noah is going to give his testimony!"

I've been in some awesome worship services at our church. Maybe you were privileged to attend the Promise Keepers event in Washington, D.C. several years ago, when more than one million men gathered to worship on the Mall. Or perhaps another powerful worship experience sticks in your memory. Think about how great it will be to participate in your first worship service in heaven. Millions of believers will be gathered together in worship. There will be no distractions, no inhibitions, and no skeptics—just the pouring out of our hearts in the power of the Holy Spirit as we praise God together. Then all will grow quiet as Jesus Christ walks to the front of the crowd and begins to teach the truths of God. How thrilling to hear from the Son himself explanations of the things of God we've never understood before. Like the two on the road to Emmaus, we'll say, "Were not our hearts burning within us while he...opened the Scriptures to us?" (Luke 24:32). I can't wait for that!

LOVED ONES AND RELATIVES WHO DIED IN CHRIST WILL BE THERE

John wrote, "Before me was a great multitude that no one could count, from every nation, tribe, people and language, standing before the throne and in front of the Lamb" (Revelation 7:9). There will be lots of interesting people to meet and enjoy in heaven. (When I hear people complain that our church is "too big," I want to tell them they're going to hate heaven!) But not only will there be new people to meet. As the old song says, "Friends will be there I have loved long ago."

For years I've taught a men's Bible study on Saturday mornings. Once I asked the older men whether they feared death more or less as they aged. They all agreed that even though death grew closer every day, they feared it less. "Why is that?" I asked. Butch Dabney said, "Because you have more friends in heaven than you've got on earth."

People ask me, "Do you really think we'll know each other in heaven? Will I recognize my friends and family members?" Jesus told the penitent thief on the cross, "Today you will be with me in paradise" (Luke 23:43). That sounds like Jesus expected to recognize him. When Moses and Elijah appeared with Jesus on the Mount of Transfiguration, the disciples knew who they were, even though they had lived centuries before. The followers of Christ recognized him in his resurrected body.

Imagine the reunion that will take place in heaven. I so look forward to seeing my dad there. I know people who look

205

forward to seeing their children again or a mate who has already crossed over to the other side. Others long to see a grandparent, a sibling, or an old friend. That's why heaven is called "home." It's where loved ones are.

Years ago my family moved out of a house we had lived in for twenty years. I thought I was really going to miss that old place. But I never did. It was easy to adjust to the new house because that's where my family lived. It's the relationships, not a certain location, that make a place home. Heaven is a place we've never been before, but our Father is there; and the older we get, the more loved ones we have waiting there to welcome us. It won't take long for heaven to feel like home.

REWARDS AND HONOR WILL BE THERE

Jesus promised, "The Son of Man is going to come in his Father's glory with his angels, and then he will reward each person according to what he has done" (Matthew 16:27). We are saved by grace, but we'll be rewarded in heaven for our works. Heaven is not portrayed in Scripture as a place of bland equality. Though everyone will be eternally happy in heaven (there will be no more sorrow), some will be rewarded and honored more than others. Paul warned:

> If any man builds on this foundation using gold, silver, costly stones, wood, hay or straw, his work will be shown for what it is, because the Day will bring it to light. It will be revealed with fire, and the fire will test the quality of

each man's work. If what he has built survives, he will receive his reward. If it is burned up, he will suffer loss; he himself will be saved, but only as one escaping through the flames. (1 Corinthians 3:12–15)

The coach of a winning ball team might hold an awards banquet at which he recognizes each player as being a special part of the team but gives special honor to the players who have worked hardest and contributed most.

In the same way, every believer will be rewarded with salvation in heaven; but God will give special honor to some. A preacher like the apostle Paul, who endured hardships and still contributed greatly to the kingdom of God, will receive a greater reward than someone like Bob Russell, who has had it relatively easy. The Christian teenager who kept herself pure despite luring temptations will be rewarded more than the one who yielded to temptation but later repented. The godly husband who faithfully cared for his wife with Alzheimer's disease will receive a greater reward than the husband whose wife was in good health, and he took her for granted. The couple that generously gave 20 percent of their income will have more treasure stored up in heaven than the couple that just gave God the leftovers.

STUDY AND LEARNING WILL BE THERE

Some people think that as soon as we get to heaven, we will immediately know everything. That's not true. We'll never possess all knowledge, or we would be as great as

God. The Bible says there are things even the angels don't know. "Even angels long to look into these things," Peter wrote (1 Peter 1:12). Jesus said that not even the angels know what day he is returning—not even the Son himself (see Matthew 24:36). We were created a little lower than the angels, so if the angels are still learning, it stands to reason the same thing will be true for us in heaven.

Paul said, "God raised us up with Christ and seated us with him in the heavenly realms in Christ Jesus, in order that in the coming ages he might show the incomparable riches of his grace" (Ephesians 2:6–7). The word *show* in this passage means "to reveal in an ongoing, progressive way."

This is one of the things that excites me most about heaven. We'll have a greater capacity to learn and more opportunity to study. There's so much I want to learn!

I recently saw the Grand Canyon for the first time. I don't buy the theory that it took millions of years for the Colorado River to slice out that eight-mile-wide, half-mile-deep gash in the earth's surface. I want to ask God how that happened: Was it the Flood, or did you create it that way? Or was it something else?

I have some other questions I look forward to asking God too: Why didn't you get rid of Satan earlier? What did you mean when you said in Ephesians 1:5 that we are "predestined" to be adopted as sons? What role did September 11, 2001, have in your plan for the world? Why didn't the Cubs ever win a World Series?

Studying God's universe—or universes—will be so exciting with alert minds, keen memories, and the Creator himself as the teacher!

BEAUTY AND TRAVEL WILL BE THERE

John wrote, "I saw the Holy City, the new Jerusalem, coming down out of heaven from God, prepared as a bride beautifully dressed for her husband" (Revelation 21:2). The city at the center of heaven is huge. It's described in Revelation 21 as a cube, with each side measuring fourteen hundred miles. If it were placed on top of the United States, it would stretch from California to the Appalachian Mountains and from Canada to Mexico. Its highest level is five hundred times higher than the tallest mountain on earth. Gates on each side will stand wide open, which indicates there will be constant coming and going. There will be a new heaven and new earth to explore (see 2 Peter 3:13; Revelation 21:1).

Mike Breaux, the pastor at Southland Christian Church in Lexington, Kentucky, says, "God just took six days to create the earth. Jesus said, 'I go to prepare a place for you,' and he's taken nearly two thousand years to prepare it. You do the math! It's going to be spectacular!"

The Grand Canyon, Niagara Falls, Pike's Peak, the Sea of Galilee, Kanapalli Beach in Hawaii...all are just sneak previews, foretastes of glory divine that await us in heaven. In describing heaven, the Bible speaks of water, trees, light, fruit, and even animals—horses, lambs, harmless wolves, tame lions, and nonthreatening snakes.

Have you ever gone snorkeling? When you look out over the ocean from above the surface, all you see is water. But you get a snorkeling mask and some fins and put your face down in that water, suddenly a whole new world opens up to you: colorful fish, impressive plants, coral reefs. Similarly, another world in a different dimension—one infinitely more fascinating and beautiful—is waiting beyond the grave for you to explore and enjoy one day.

WORK AND ACCOMPLISHMENT WILL BE THERE

Sometimes heaven is referred to as a place of rest. That has led some to think of heaven as nothing but eternal rest—a place where we sit around on clouds and get served by angels. If you're tired and looking forward to that place of rest, then you need to know that in heaven, you'll get all the rest you need. You'll never be rushed, stressed, burned out, or emotionally exhausted. But heaven is not just eternal rest. Work and achievement will be part of our lives in heaven. The Bible says, "No longer will there be any curse. The throne of God and of the Lamb will be in the city, and his servants will serve him" (Revelation 22:3).

The curse Adam was given in the garden was not work but painful toil. Even before the Fall, Adam had work to do. He had to name the animals, take care of the garden, and harvest fruit to eat. Heaven is portrayed as a similar paradise. The curse of exhausting, frustrating, meaningless toil will be eliminated. In its place will be service rendered for Christ that will be refreshing and productive.

Have you ever engaged in a task that you absolutely loved? Maybe it was writing a lesson, tinkering with an automobile, or designing a computer program. Maybe it was coaching a ball team during an important game or singing in a concert in front of a large crowd. Were you amazed at how fast the time went by? You probably caught yourself thinking, *Where did the time go? I can't believe it's been so long! Time flies when you're having fun!* Imagine what it will be like when the God of the universe, the one who created you and knows you better than you know yourself, assigns you the very task for which you were created—the one in which you find so much fulfillment that time absolutely flies by.

The Bible says that we will judge, rule, and reign with Christ. We'll be the caretakers of the new heaven and new earth, so there will be lots of work to do. I imagine that the most meaningful rest we can experience will happen at the end of the day, when we stop and look at what we've done and hear the Lord say, "Well done, good and faithful servants! Let's go enjoy ourselves at the wedding supper of the Lamb!"

JOY AND LAUGHTER WILL BE THERE

Jesus promised, "Blessed are you who hunger now, for you will be satisfied. Blessed are you who weep now, for you will laugh" (Luke 6:21). There will be no laughter in hell. The Bible describes hell as a place of "weeping and gnashing of teeth" (Matthew 13:42). Heaven, on the other hand, will be a place of joy and laughter. Jesus said that even now there is rejoicing in heaven—whenever a sinner repents (see Luke 15:7). The Bible says that faithful servants will be welcomed into heaven by the Lord himself with the words, "Come and share your master's happiness" (Matthew 25:21).

One humorous poet described heaven as a place where there would be...

> *No dust, no rust, no rats, no rot,*
> *No raucous rock, no potent pot,*
> *No growing old with weakened sight,*
> *No dentures slipping when you bite,*
> *No bombs, no guns, no courts, no jails,*
> *Where all succeed and no one fails,*
> *No strikes, no layoffs, full employment,*
> *And everyone with job enjoyment,*
> *All tell the truth, state only facts,*
> *No wars, no debts, no income tax.*
> *According to this dream of mine,*
> *In heaven no one stands in line*
> *And there are only smiling faces*
> *And lots and lots of parking places.*[4]

One of the things I love about our church is that it's a place where people laugh. I wish you could have heard them laugh recently when I told them about a funny thing that happened to me. Our new addition to the preaching team, Kyle Idleman, has been a big hit in our congregation. Everyone is talking about how he preaches without notes—

how he memorizes every word of his manuscript and preaches for thirty minutes *without notes.*

I told the congregation I was getting a little sick of hearing about this new preacher who preaches *without notes.* Then I got an invitation to go with Coach Denny Crum to the John Wooden Classic—a college basketball tournament held in Indianapolis in honor of Coach John Wooden. Coach Wooden, the legendary UCLA basketball coach, was Denny Crum's mentor and has always been a hero of mine, a great Christian man who is now in his nineties. Coach Crum said, "Bob, if you go with me, I'll introduce you to John Wooden."

Well, I thought, *I hate to miss our Saturday night service, but Kyle's preaching that weekend, and at least I won't have to stand around after church and hear about the guy who preaches without notes!* So I told Kyle a few days beforehand that I wouldn't be present on Saturday night because I was going to Indianapolis to meet John Wooden.

"Tell him I said hello," Kyle said.

"Oh, you know John Wooden?" I asked.

"Yes. He's a member at Shepherd of the Hills." (That's the church that helped Kyle start his congregation in southern California. Kyle preached there once a month for a year.)

When I met John Wooden, we exchanged a few pleasantries, and then I said, "By the way, Kyle Idleman said to tell you hello."

And you guessed it—this is not an exaggeration—Coach

Wooden said, "Kyle Idleman! He's the only guy I've ever heard preach *without notes!*"

You can imagine how much our congregation enjoyed that story. And I enjoyed telling it because they are such good laughers. A couple of years ago, a professional broadcaster called our church to find out what company we got our laugh track from. He had heard my sermons on the radio and loved the "genuine-sounding" laughter in the background. Was he ever surprised when he heard we didn't use a laugh track. The reason it sounded genuine is that it is genuine!

You can be sure there will be lots of laughter—and no need for a laugh track—in heaven.

ACTIVITIES AND ADVENTURE WILL BE THERE

Have you ever been to Disney World with young children? You're immediately surrounded with opportunity for activity and adventure. Mickey Mouse and Goofy come to greet you, parades come by with bands playing, rides call out to you from every corner. You can hardly control the children's excitement. Then you're given a brochure with several different "kingdoms" you can visit. You begin to realize that there's so much to do, you can't do it all in one day. Your kids want to ride the rides and visit the animals. You want to see a couple of shows and eat at a certain restaurant. If only you had more time to explore.

One of my favorite word pictures of heaven is this: Jesus

said, "In my Father's house are many rooms" (John 14:2). One of them has your name on it—it's your special room, your place that Jesus has prepared just for you. Don't you wonder what it might be like? I'm sure it will be perfect for you.

And don't you wonder what some of the other rooms in the Father's house are like?

I think there will be a question-and-answer room, where you can go to get some of your most complex questions answered.

One room is surely a dining room. The Bible promises that we'll sit down with the Lord at the wedding supper of the Lamb, where a great feast of rich food is waiting (see Isaiah 25:6). And there you can eat to your heart's content without worrying about calories, carbohydrates, cholesterol, or fat. Guilt-free eating in the dining room of God!

I wonder if there will be an instant-replay room where you can replay certain moments of history and see how they actually occurred. You can watch the Creation, the Flood, David killing Goliath, Jesus' resurrection, the American Revolution, and so on. You could even watch a replay of your life—what it looked like from God's perspective. Of course, certain parts will have been edited out!

Maybe there will be a music room where you can listen to the greatest ensembles, bands, soloists, choirs, and orchestras ever assembled.

I picture a craft and hobby room where you can learn to do some of the things you didn't have time to do on earth:

photography, scuba diving, rebuilding old cars, scrapbooking, or flying an airplane.

Surely there will be a sermon room where you can hear the greatest preachers in history. You can look at the schedule and say, "Let's go hear Billy Sunday today and Martin Luther tomorrow." Your kids will say, "Let's do that next millennium!"

I imagine a recreation room where you sign up for fishing trips, snow skiing trips, and opportunities to play golf courses that make Augusta National look like a cheap municipal course.

Most of this speculating probably sounds pretty immature to the God who knows all things. But he did encourage us to set our minds on things above, so I'm sure he's not offended. Still, the real heaven is so much greater than I've described. The Bible says that God is "able to do immeasurably more than all we ask or imagine" (Ephesians 3:20). But this one thing I know for sure about heaven...

JESUS CHRIST, THE RESURRECTED SAVIOR, WILL BE THERE

Jesus said, "If I go and prepare a place for you, I will come back and take you to be with me that you also may be where I am" (John 14:3). What will it be like to have a one-on-one meeting with Jesus Christ? What will it be like to stand before Jesus, to see the nail scars in his hands as his arms are extended, to witness the smile on his face, and to hear these words from his lips: "Well done...welcome home"? What will it be like to see him face to face and say, "Lord, I don't deserve to be here. I can't believe you loved me enough to die for me after all I've done. But Jesus, I just want to thank you for your amazing grace, for being so good, for dying for me"?

Lord, when I pray, help me to pray with eternity in mind.

I can only imagine.

NOTES

CHAPTER ONE

1. Some will be quick to ask, "But what about those verses like 1 Samuel 15:29 which say that God does not change his mind?" The same Hebrew word is used—*nacham*—in Exodus 32:14 (God *changed his mind*) and in 1 Samuel 15:29 (God cannot *change his mind*). To reconcile these two passages, some theologians claim that the passage about God changing his mind is to be taken metaphorically, similar to the "strong arm of God" being metaphorical for God himself. God knows what he is going to do, but to relate his grace in human terms, he "pretends" to promise to destroy the entire nation. But if God is pretending, then God is promising something he has no intention of carrying out, so we are still left with God being untruthful. The context of 1 Samuel 15:29 indicates that what God cannot do is lie or break a promise: God "does not lie or change his mind," Samuel said. Once God has promised or vowed to do something, it will be done. There is an assumption then in Exodus 32 that God is not promising but threatening. "I will destroy these people," God is threatening, "unless you care enough to convince me otherwise, Moses."

If God has the freedom to change his mind without lying in cases where he has not made a vow but a threat (in the same way that a human can change his mind without lying), then we are left to believe that Moses—and we—can truly change God's mind just as the passage indicates.

2. For an excellent critique of open theism, see Bruce Ware, *God's Lesser Glory: The Diminished God of Open Theism* (Wheaton, Ill.: Crossway Books, 2000). Dr. Ware is a moderate Calvinist, and I don't agree with his (very slight) criticism of classical Arminianism. However, his treatment is fair, and Calvinists and Arminians agree that Dr. Ware's assault on open theism is justified and well done.

3. *Back to the Future, Part 2*, dir. Robert Zemeckis, Universal Studios, 1989.

4. Reuters News Service, quoted by Softrom.net news, October 7, 2002. See http://www.softrom.net/news/details. asp?NewsID=31.

5. C. S. Lewis, *Miracles* (New York: MacMillan Publishing Co., 1960), 179.

6. Bruce Wilkinson, *The Prayer of Jabez: Breaking Through to the Blessed Life* (Sisters, Ore.: Multnomah Publishers, 2000), 49–52.

7. Patrick Morley, *The Man in the Mirror* (Grand Rapids: Zondervan, 1997), 116–17.

8. Max Lucado, *America Looks Up* (Nashville: W Publishing Group, 2002), 64–65.

CHAPTER TWO

1. Jeanie Davis, "The Power of Prayer in Medicine: People Who Are Prayed for Fare Better," *Journal of Reproductive Health*, September 2001 (Copyright WebMD Corp. 2001), http://mywebmd.com/content/

article/35/1728_92943.htm?lastselectedguid={5FE84E90-BC77-4056-A91C-9531713CA348}.

2. Norman Geisler, *Miracles and Modern Thought* (Grand Rapids: Zondervan, 1982), 13.

3. C. S. Lewis, *Miracles*, 15.

4. Matthew 12:24; see also Acts 4:16, where the enemies of the apostles admit they can't deny that a miracle has been done.

CHAPTER THREE

1. Warren Wiersbe, *The Bible Exposition Commentary, New Testament*, vol. 2 (Colorado Springs: Victor Publishing, 2001), 383.

2. Charles H. Spurgeon in L. B. Cowan, *Streams in the Desert* (Grand Rapids: Zondervan, 1925), November 17 entry.

3. Jim Patillo, "God Sold the Cattle," *Wit and Wisdom* (September 1998), www.witandwisdom.org/archive/1998 0929. htm.

CHAPTER FOUR

1. Some theologians might argue that God knew he was going to change his mind, so he didn't really change his mind. I agree that God knew he was going to change his mind, because as we discussed in chapter 3, God knew what he would do if Hezekiah didn't pray (let him die) and what he would do if he did pray (heal him). God knew Hezekiah was going to pray, so he knew he was going to change his mind. But this doesn't alter the fact that God did change his mind. I might say to my grandson, "Let's go to Cracker Barrel to eat." I'm thinking that if he asks to go to McDonald's instead, I'll let him change my mind. And I know with an almost absolute certainty that he's going to respond, "Pop, I'd

really rather go to McDonald's." Do I still "change my mind"? Yes. I planned to change my mind, and I didn't actually change my mind until he asked. He had the choice not to change my mind, even though I was certain he would attempt to. The analogy breaks down only slightly when you consider that I don't have perfect foreknowledge. (Although in that case, it would be nearly perfect.)

2. John McRay, "Christian History 47," in Elesha Coffman, *Christianity Today*. Web site:http://www.christianitytoday.com/history/newsletter/2002/may31.html.

CHAPTER FIVE

1. Charles R. Swindoll, *Bible Study Guide: James* (Fullerton, Calif.: Insight for Living, 1983), 84.

2. Rachel Clark, "Arizona Fire Leaves Long-Term Burden," *Disaster News Network* (23 September 2002), http://www.disasternews.net/news/news.php?articleid=1572. Information about the three crosses came from direct correspondence with the mission when we contacted them for verification of this story.

3. Summary of "Adrift," © 1992 by Sandra Barker. Used by permission.

4. Terry Mattingly, "Prayer and Action," *World*, 9 November 2002.

5. Ibid.

6. Ron DeMarco, "Dreams," © 1999 Ron DeMarco and friend, http://angelart-gallery.com/forum/demarco.html.

CHAPTER SIX

1. Paul Marshall, *Their Blood Cries Out: The Untold Story of Persecution Against Christians in the Modern World* (Dallas: Word Publishing, 1997), from a summary on the back of the book.

2. dc talk, *Jesus Freaks* (Tulsa, Okla.: Albury Publishing, 1999), inside cover.

3. U.S. House Resolution, Scripps-Howard News Service (28 September 1996).

4. Elizabeth P. Prentiss, "More Love to Thee." Music by William H. Doane. Public Domain.

5. dc talk, *Jesus Freaks* (Tulsa, OK: Albury Publishing, 1999), 124–25.

6. Bob Russell, "A Call for National Repentance," *Lookout Magazine* (Cincinnati: Standard Publishing), 5 November 1995.

7. "Franklin's Appeal for Prayer at the Constitutional Convention." Available from http://www.wallbuilders.com/resources/search/detail. php?ResourceID=19.

CHAPTER SEVEN

1. We don't know why the disciples couldn't drive out the demon, but perhaps it was their overconfidence. Later they asked Jesus why they weren't successful and Jesus said, "This kind comes out only by prayer." It sounds like the disciples forgot to pray!

CHAPTER EIGHT

1. C. S. Lewis, *The World's Last Night and Other Essays* (New York: Harcourt, Brace, and Company, 1952), 10.

2. Warren Wiersbe, *The Bible Exposition Commentary, New Testament*, vol. 1 (Colorado Springs: Victor Publishing, 2001), 676.

3. Dallas Willard, *The Divine Conspiracy: Rediscovering Hidden Life in God* (HarperSanFrancisco, a division of HarperCollins Publishers, 1998), 340.

4. Oswald Chambers, *My Utmost for His Highest: An Updated Edition*

in Today's Language (Grand Rapids: Discovery House Publishers, 1992), August 24 entry.

CHAPTER NINE

1. "Unanswered Prayers" performed by Garth Brooks, written by Patrick Alger, Larry B. Bastian, and Troyal Garth Brooks. © 1991 Major Bob Music/Mid-Summer Music, Inc./Universal Music Publishing Group/Universal Polygram International Publishing, Inc. c/o Universal Music Publishing Group. All rights reserved.

2. J. Wallace Hamilton, *Where Now Is Thy God?* (Old Tappan, N. J.: Fleming H. Revell Company, 1969), 46–47.

CHAPTER TEN

1. Elisabeth Elliot, *A Heart for God* (Lincoln, Nebr.: Gateway to Joy Publishers, 1995).

2. C. S. Lewis, *Mere Christianity* (New York: Macmillan Publishing Company, 1943), 120.

3. The early Christians referred to our atmosphere surrounding this earth as the first heaven, the stars and galaxies above as the second heaven, and the place where God dwells as the third heaven.

4. Source unknown.